I Read It,
but
I Don't Get It

Comprehension Strategies for Adolescent Readers

Cris Tovani

SMOKY HILL HIGH SCHOOL, AURORA, COLORADO

Foreword by Ellin Oliver Keene

Stenhouse Publishers Portland, Maine

Stenhouse Publishers
www.stenhouse.com

Credits

Page 18: Adapted from the Public Education and Business Coalition's (PEBC) Literacy Platform. Copyright © 2000. Reprinted by permission of the PEBC, Denver, Colorado.

Page 25: Home buyer/robber story from J. W. Pichert and R. C. Anderson, "Taking Different Perspectives on a Story." Copyright © 1977. *Journal of Educational Psychology* 69 (4): 309–315. Reprinted by permission.

Page 68: "Valentine for Ernest Mann," by Naomi Shihab Nye, from *Red Suitcase.* Copyright © 1994. Reprinted by permission of the author.

Page 71: From *If I Die in a Combat Zone,* by Tim O'Brien, copyright © 1973 by Tim O'Brien. Used by permission of Dell Publishing, a division of Random House, Inc.

Library of Congress Cataloging-in-Publication Data
Tovani, Cris.
    I read it, but I don't get it : comprehension strategies for adolescent readers / Cris Tovani ; foreword by Ellin Keene.
    p.   cm.
    Includes bibliographical references (p.).
    ISBN 1-57110-089-X
    1. Reading comprehension. 2. Reading (Secondary) 3. Reading—Remedial teaching I. Title: Comprehension strategies for adolescent readers. II. Title.
    LB1050.45.T68 2000
    428.4'3—dc21   00-058798

Interior design by Ron Kosciak, Dragonfly Design
Cover design by Martha Drury

Manufactured in the United States of America on acid-free paper
05 04 03 02   9 8 7

To my first and finest teachers, Mom and Dad

Contents

Foreword

Have you ever found yourself in a spot—perhaps a deserted stretch of beach, hiking through untouched snow, in the midst of a great city swirling with energy, or in a museum new to you where you first lay eyes on a painting that brings a lump to your throat—and you get the sense that you are home, that you belong? It is rare that we experience that sense of being home in a professional setting, but that is exactly what I experience when I am in Cris Tovani's classroom.

Welcome home. *I Read It, but I Don't Get It* is going to sound very close to home if you work with middle and high school kids. It is going to make you remember all over again why you love these kids and this work so much. And it's going to equip you with a huge cache of new ways to approach and extend the kids' comprehension, whether they are reading the lunch menu or Tolstoy.

Throughout my first reading of this book, I asked myself, How can Cris nail it like this? How can she record so perfectly the experiences, the frustrations, and the hilarity of working with middle and high school kids? Even more astonishing, how can she make me flash back across the years (many, believe me) to find my teenaged self slumped in a chair, smirking and getting ready to "fake out Mrs. Fill-in-the-Blank" with how I had read the assigned book or the dreaded selection from the English anthology and understood it so well that I could nod knowingly and look thoughtful enough not to be called on?

Cris can nail it because she deeply understands and cares about adolescents and because she understands reading, inside out, upside down, and backwards. That's a powerful combination in this era when so many students have applied their considerable intellectual capacity and energy to fake-read for the whole of their school lives. We can all recall dozens, maybe even hundreds, of upper elementary, middle, and high school students who read fluently, pronounce words magnificently and have very little notion of the meaning, to say nothing of insight, about what they've just read. What can be done to help these kids? Is it too late?

How do we find ourselves in this quagmire? How is it that thousands of middle and high school students can read words but struggle to construct meaning? I am reminded of a book I read on parenting when my daughter was a toddler. In a particularly memorable passage, the distinguished pediatrician/author was asked by desperate parents why their child still didn't sleep through the night at age three. The doctor said simply that children get good at what they are taught. These parents had inadvertently taught their child that waking up in the middle of the night would be rewarded with milk, rocking, singing, cuddling, and eventually sleeping with Mom and Dad.

In this country, our children have gotten really good at what they have been taught. They come into elementary school desperate to please their teachers, who teach them to read words well. The children, for the most part, learn to do well what they are taught. Juxtapose that scenario on the increasing call for kids to solve complex problems, work in cooperative groups to create original products following lengthy research, synthesize information from a wide variety of sources, and communicate their findings concisely and persuasively. How are we teaching the kids to undertake these challenges? In this book we see that if kids are taught how to think they learn and demonstrate that learning in increasingly complex situations.

In *I Read It, but I Don't Get It,* Cris shows that the Jims and Kadees and Leighas (you'll meet them all!) of this world can be taught to read and comprehend with depth and, you're not going to believe this until you read the book, zeal. I said zeal. This book reveals how Cris's honesty and humor translate into a challenge to kids to find their own capacity to think while they read. Cris shows how thinking comes to life in classes as disparate as World Literature and reader's workshop. She shows how, through thinking aloud and other powerful teaching strategies, we can teach kids to manipulate their own thinking in order to understand more completely.

Cris doesn't coddle you any more than she coddles the kids in her second-hour class. She makes it clear that if you are looking for one-shot solutions, easy remedies, and step-by-step processes to implement mindlessly, this is not the book for you. Cris clearly acknowledges the challenges teachers face in working with reluctant readers and, interestingly, readers who have had tremendous success in school without ever thinking deeply about what they read. Yet she minces no words in saying, dear reader, this is our responsibility. This is a kindergarten through grade 12 issue and all of us, no matter the grade or content area we teach, can and must tackle it.

In each chapter, Cris introduces you to her students and recounts conversations, body language, and noises from the kids that will make you laugh out loud. And with a one-two punch Cris hits you with dozens of workable ideas that have succeeded in her own classroom. What more can we ask for than chapters that end with a What Works section? Don't miss the teaching points in these sections. They are, taken collectively, some of the finest strategies for comprehension that I have ever read.

Building on research that clearly defines thinking strategies proficient readers use to comprehend, Cris shows how she has taught kids to probe more deeply, think more profoundly, reflect, and struggle for insight. She takes us beyond the superficial to show how hard kids work when the reward is internal: the gratification that comes from discovering their own intellectual capacity.

Cris is a teacher of teachers as well as of kids. During her time at the Public Education and Business Coalition (PEBC) in Denver, working as a staff developer with teachers in kindergarten through grade 12 in highly impacted urban areas and affluent suburbs, Cris gathered and refined hundreds of teaching strategies that she brings to her work with kids. That range of experience, in addition to exposing her to hundreds of teachers and their marvelous work, teaches us that we have far, far more in common than our grade and departmental, urban and suburban designations may suggest. Cris teaches us that kids of any age and background who are treated with respect, trusted to be brilliant, and shown how to be more proficient readers and writers, will dramatically surpass our highest expectations.

Does Cris succeed in the classroom? As a staff developer? Superbly. That is why she gets it so right in this book. She knows these kids, she knows reading, and she knows that we can help all kids comprehend deeply and remember that which matters most, to them and to their eventual participation in this democracy.

Have you ever found yourself in a spot—perhaps a deserted stretch of beach, hiking through untouched snow, in the midst of a great city swirling with energy, or in a museum new to you where you first lay eyes on a painting that brings a lump to your throat—and you get the sense that you are home, that you belong? Is it possible to think of your classroom that way? Is it possible to turn on the lights in your room every morning knowing that the students with whom you work will understand more than any you've worked with? Wouldn't it be extraordinary to be in a profession where you felt like that, where those with whom you work are thriving? Welcome home. You've chosen the right career. You've chosen the right book.

Ellin Oliver Keene
August 2000

Acknowledgments

Number seven on my list of things to do before I die was "write a book." It was an accomplishment that I didn't really think I'd achieve, but thanks to a lot of people, this book has become a reality.

First, my heartfelt thanks goes to Stephanie Harvey, who brought Philippa Stratton, my editor from Stenhouse, into my classroom on a cold February day to watch me teach. Stephanie encouraged me to write about my students so other teachers could see what was happening in my classroom. Throughout this process she has been my mentor, my teacher, and most of all my friend.

Second, I'd like to thank Ellin Keene for pursuing her work in reading comprehension. Never before have I met a person who can synthesize research into practical application like she does. I admire her intelligence and her ability to lead and guide the training team at the Public Education and Business Coalition (PEBC). Ellin's work has inspired me to take risks. Her role as a provocateur has forced me continually to question what it is I do as a teacher.

And these thank-yous as well:

—To Chryse Hutchins, for the many hours she spent in my room observing and scripting students' conversations. Her humility and willingness to share ideas, observations, and kudos encouraged me to keep going when the end was not in sight. Chryse's uncanny ability to put words to thinking has allowed me to re-create, revamp, and rethink many lessons that failed.

—To Dee Bench, my friend and reading partner and wonderful sounding board, for taking budding ideas and shaping them into reality.

—To Anne Goudvis, for her wisdom and skill at finding any research citation I needed.

—To Mariah Dickson, for her ability to listen and support the work I do in the classroom.

—To Susan Zimmermann, for her insight and leadership.

—To Philippa Stratton, for her encouragement and wonderful sense of humor.

—To Brenda Power, for her wisdom and gentle nudges to "get finished."

—To Colleen Buddy, whose lessons and metaphors I use throughout this book.

—To Laura Benson, my first PEBC trainer, who helped start Cherry Creek School District's Secondary Reading Project (SRP).

—To Barbara Volpe, current director of PEBC, and Judy Hendricks, administrative assistant at PEBC, who take care of the details and never forget the larger vision.

—To Roseanne Ridgley, my first teammate at Smoky Hill High and my partner in SRP.

—To Bonnie Kelly and Denise Campbell, who continue to work with me as staff developers in Cherry Creek. Their organization keeps me on track and my feet on the ground.

—To Dr. Mary Jarvis, whose courage allowed her to hire a first-grade teacher to teach struggling high school readers. I thank her for trusting my work and supporting me in my staff development endeavors.

—To Nola Wellman and Terry Conley, whose foresight allowed Cherry Creek School to investigate and solve the problems of secondary readers.

—To my friends and colleagues, who worked with me on the Secondary Reading Project. You guys are true pros.

—To Marlene Davis, for her hours spent editing nonsensical early drafts.

—To Laura Witmer, who when the panic was greatest, helped me transfer the manuscript to a real computer.

—To my mom, who taught me how to love books and that there was more to a story than sounding out the words.

—To my dad, who taught me anything is possible with persistence.

—To my three brothers, who were bragging about this book long before it was written.

—To my three daughters, Rhiannon, Sara, and Caroline, who have humored me as I experimented on them with new ideas. Thank you for giving me feedback about books and classroom activities. (A special thank-you to Caroline, my youngest, who has taken a backseat while this book was being written. Her kisses and hugs as I sat at the computer gave me the energy to continue.)

—To my husband, Pete, who is always searching for reading material he thinks might interest the readers who hate to read. The fruits of his searches have supported many of my classroom ideas. Most of all I thank him for driving carpools, coaching basketball, braiding hair, fixing meals, and rubbing my shoulders late at night as I tried to finish chapters. His encouragement and incredible support allowed me to continue teaching full time while I wrote this book. I couldn't have a better partner.

And last to the many students who shared their thinking and allowed me to learn from them. I am grateful to have been their teacher.

1 Fake Reading

"This is reading workshop, and I am Cris Tovani. You are in Room 11, and it's now fourth hour. Please check your schedules to make sure you are in the right place. If you're not, I'll be happy to help you find where you need to be."

"Miss," a kid from the back calls, "my schedule's wrong. I'm supposed to have weight training fourth hour, not reading workshop."

"Yeah," another chimes in. "I signed up for pottery, not reading."

"Well, I know," I stammer. "Many of your schedules were changed over the summer. For some reason your elective was replaced with my class, reading workshop."

"Are you telling me I can't read?" accuses a large girl next to the door.

"Actually, I have no idea what kind of reader you are, but someone has recommended that you take this class." Rumblings of discontent circulate through the room. I attempt to shift the focus. "We'll figure out who gets to stay and who has to leave after today. For now, just hold tight and we'll deal with schedule changes tomorrow."

I continue taking roll.

"Jim Anderson."

"Yeah, right here."

"Justin Baldwin."

"Here."

"Theresa Black. Theresa Black? Is Theresa Black here?"

"Oh, that's me."

"Leigha Collins?"

"Leigha's not coming today. She says there's no way she's taking another reading class. She's dropping."

"Great," I mumble to myself. It's the first day of school and kids are already dropping courses. I know if I can just get them to class, I might have a shot at helping them improve their reading comprehension.

1

Unfortunately, they're disappointed by their schedules, expecting one class and getting another. Their attitudes stink, and I have more than a sneaking suspicion they have the wrong idea about this course. It's probably very different from remedial reading classes they've had in the past.

Ever since I could read words, I've wanted to know what else a person had to do in order to make sense of text. I didn't have a problem decoding. I had a problem understanding. I faked comprehension for years. I knew it would eventually catch up with me. But I didn't know what to do. I thought I was just born a bad reader. It was a great relief to learn there was something I could do to improve my comprehension. It's no wonder I have dedicated my life to helping readers much like myself make sense of text.

My first job as a teacher was in a posh suburban neighborhood. I was working with twenty-four second graders. Only two of them could read. I didn't know how to teach reading, and I immediately started a master's degree program in reading at the University of Colorado. I was fortunate to be taught by Pat Hagerty for much of my degree program. She introduced me to the work of Frank Smith and Ken Goodman, to schema theory, and to the interactive model of reading. I soon discovered that learning how to teach kids to read wasn't going to be a semester-long adventure but rather a lifelong pursuit.

My second year found me in a more diverse neighborhood. I was teaching third and fourth graders. Many of them could read the words but couldn't make sense of what they were reading. About the time I finished my master's degree, I became involved with a nonprofit organization that at the time was called the Public Education Coalition. It later merged with another organization and became known as the Public Education and Business Coalition (PEBC).

Susan Zimmermann, cofounder of PEBC, hired me as a trainer. For the last twelve years I have had the pleasure of working with an incredible group of people. I left the classroom for three of those years, working as a staff developer. Then I decided it was time to return to the classroom and try some of the ideas I was asking teachers all over the Denver metropolitan area to try.

The work of PEBC has been quite successful with elementary schoolchildren. PEBC leaders and staff developers have written two widely acclaimed books about teaching comprehension in workshop settings—*Mosaic of Thought*, by Ellin Keene and Susan Zimmermann (Heinemann 1997), and *Strategies That Work*, by Stephanie Harvey and Anne Goudvis (Stenhouse 2000). As part of the team that helped develop these strategies, I wanted to see whether they could work with adolescent readers of all ages and ability levels. I applied at Smoky Hill High School (2,800 students in a culturally diverse, middle-class suburb) and got the job of reading specialist and English teacher.

And that's how I came to be calling roll on the first day of reading workshop.

Establishing Expectations

In their methods courses, teachers-to-be learn to set expectations, make them clear, and keep them simple. Before I share what I expect of students, I want to know what they expect from reading workshop.

Hurrying through roll, I quickly pass out half sheets of paper. I ask the students to jot down what they expect to learn from the class. Surprisingly, they write with vigor. It seems almost cathartic for some. I stop them after five minutes and ask them to share what they have written.

"We have to share these out loud?" a kid in the back asks.

"Yeah," I say. "What's the big deal?"

"Well, you're not actually gonna tell us if we're right or wrong, are you?"

"Right about what?" I ask.

"Right about what we think is going to happen in here," he says.

"I'll tell you if what you think is going to happen is actually going to happen. Okay?"

A snotty voice next to the potted plant says, "I bet we'll be doing lots of book reports in here. I hate book reports."

"Me too," I say. "If you think you hate doing them, try grading twenty-eight of the boring things." Five heads snap up and deliver skeptical looks. I continue. "Book reports are so dumb. Most kids, by the time they are in second grade, know how to cheat on one. I even cheated when I had to do them. Anybody want to know how I got away with it?" By this time, every student in the class is staring at me with mouth slightly agape, not quite believing a teacher is going to tell them how to cheat. "Well, it isn't that tough. You probably have a million better ways to cheat than I did, but this is how I did it. I'd go to the library and check out a book that looked like it hadn't been read in years. I stayed away from the classics like *Charlotte's Web* [White 1952] and *Island of the Blue Dolphins* [O'Dell 1960]—you know, the ones teachers know about. I'd pick one that seemed really boring and then I'd look at the little flap of paper on the inside of the front cover that told you when the book had to be returned. When I'd choose a book for my book report, I'd make sure no one had checked the book out for several years. Those were the best ones, since I was pretty sure no overworked teacher would spend time reading a book that unpopular. I'd read the first page, the last page, and skim the table of contents. Then I'd write the book report. Before I turned the assignment in, I'd return the book. Once it was shelved, I'd find it and put it in the wrong section so my teacher wouldn't be able to find it. It was a breeze. Sometimes I'd get that paranoid feeling that this would be the time I'd get caught. But I never did. It worked every time."

No one speaks. They all stare at me. "So," I continue, "if you think I'm going to waste my time grading book reports that most of you have faked doing, you're crazy. We have much more important work to do than that. In answer to your question, there will definitely be no book reports."

A hand from the back of the room shoots up. "What's your name?" I ask.

"Jeff," he says.

"Go ahead, Jeff."

"If you really want to cheat, make up the title of the book. Then there's no way the teacher will ever be able to tell if you read it."

I smile. "See, I thought you probably had better ways to cheat than I did."

For the next ten minutes, the students talk about how they have avoided reading for the last six years, how they think they have *pulled the wool over their teachers' eyes*. I am amazed by their caginess and impressed by the sophistication of their avoidance strategies.

One student remarks, "I haven't read a book since third grade."

Another blurts out, "Big deal, I haven't ever finished a chapter book. I've faked reading since second grade."

I hear these words, and I am reminded of myself as a young reader. I, too, was a master of fake reading.

I started to "fake-read" in sixth grade and continued doing so for the next twenty years. In high school, I fooled everyone by attending classes, reading first and last chapters, skimming through Cliffs Notes, and making Bs or better on essays and exams. My GPA wavered between a 3.2 and a 3.5. However, June of my senior year approached, and the very real possibility that I would graduate without really being able to read scared me to death. I didn't think I could get away with fake reading in college. I read aloud beautifully and could decode even the most difficult words. The problem surfaced when I had to use, remember, or retell what I had read. I couldn't do it. I expected that meaning would arrive if I could pronounce all the words. Unfortunately, that didn't happen. I figured I was just a bad reader.

I had one semester left to learn how to really read. I was determined that if I set my mind to it, I could teach myself how to read before June. I'd start learning with the next assigned English book. Unfortunately for me, it was *Heart of Darkness,* by Joseph Conrad. I tried to get "psyched": I told myself all I had to do was read the words carefully. I began with the best of intentions, with Cliffs Notes by my side to offer a second opinion. After being told that the movie *Apocalypse Now* was the modern-day version of *Heart of Darkness,* I saw it three times. At the end of the unit, I took my exam and got the usual B. To this day, I have no idea what the book is about. All the effort and hard work hadn't made a bit of difference.

I was sure I had missed a giant secret somewhere along the way. I decided to ask my teacher, Mr. Cantril, what I could do to help myself. One day after class, I got up the courage to ask him the big question: "What do you do if you read every page but still have no idea what the book is about?"

He peered over his bifocals and said, "Obviously, you weren't concentrating. Reread the book and this time pay attention."

Ha! What did he mean I wasn't concentrating? What kind of instruction was that? Pay attention! I was paying attention. I wanted to know what else I could do when reading the words didn't help. What could I do differently the second time that I hadn't already done? At the age of seventeen, I wasn't ready to concede that I was destined to be illiterate. I knew there had to be something I could do to improve my reading. In the meantime, I would have to fake-read.

"If we aren't going to do book reports, what are we going to do?" asks Jeff.

"We are going to study what good readers do," I inform them. "We're going to learn how to use thinking strategies."

For years, reading specialists identified what struggling readers did poorly and then tried to correct it. I didn't think this would work with frustrated high school readers who already thought they'd never be good readers. I believed in the work of Donald Graves and Nancie Atwell. The thinking behind the writers-workshop movement of the mid-1980s—to teach students what good writers do when writing—made sense. There wasn't any reason why the same idea couldn't be adapted to reading instruction. I would concentrate my efforts on teaching students how to do what good readers did.

"What do you mean by a strategy?" asks Kandice.

"A strategy," I tell the class, "is an intentional plan that readers use to help themselves make sense of their reading. Strategies are flexible and can be adapted to meet the demands of the reading task. Good readers use lots of strategies to help themselves make sense of text. We're going to become better readers by imitating what good readers do when they read."

"How's that going to help?" wonders Jeff.

"Think about the real world for a minute," I say. "When you are trying to learn how to do something, do you ask someone who doesn't know how to do it for help?" Not waiting for a response, I continue. "Probably not. Jeff, what do you do for fun?"

Jeff thinks for a minute and then says, "I play the bass guitar in a band."

"Great," I say. "How do you learn new songs? Do you ask your mom?"

"No," he says disgustedly.

"Well, what do you do?"

"I ask this guy Ray, who has been in a band for five years. He plays really good songs and he shows me chords and cool riffs."

"Why do you ask Ray for help?"

"Because he's good. He shows me what he's doing."

I smile. "Well, I'm going to show you what good readers do and then teach you how to do it. If you want to be a good reader, you need to figure out what good readers do and try to copy it."

The bell rings and I overhear Jeff say to a friend, "This class might not be so bad after all."

The next day, I have noticeably more students in class. Word appears to have gotten around that there are no book reports. As students file into the room, I hand each of them a yellow sticky note. I ask them to write down what they think good readers do when they read. After a minute, I notice no one is writing and everyone is staring at me. "Are you stuck?" I ask.

"We don't know what good readers do," says Courtney.

"Well, what do you do when you read?" I ask.

"I reread a lot," Courtney says.

"Write that down," I tell her. "Think about what happens to you when you read and jot that down on the sticky note."

Pencils begin to fly across the yellow squares. After a minute or two I record their responses on an overhead transparency, starting with Courtney's. A few of the strategies really can be used to improve comprehension:

reread

skip words

read slowly

But others are indicative of students who long ago gave up trying to understand difficult text:

listen to Walkman while reading

don't read for fun

fall asleep

daydream

fake-read

forget what I read

read the words without knowing what they mean

read the back of the book instead of the whole book

see the movie instead of reading the book

ask people what the book is about so I don't have to read

read without paying attention

read too fast

start books and never finish them

just look at the words

lose my place

Each trait is shared as a badge of honor; they are almost proud of this behavior. Then Courtney says something quite disturbing. "Some kids are born good readers and some kids aren't. I've always been a bad reader and I always will be. It's too late for me."

Many teachers might agree with Courtney. There are those who think good readers are created in the womb and nurtured on the laps of indulgent mothers who read nightly to their natural born readers. I once heard a middle school language arts teacher complain that she was sick and tired of trying to teach kids how to read. She hated the cliché that *all teachers are teachers of reading.* She grumbled that it was ridiculous to expect secondary teachers to teach reading when they had so much content to cover. Indignantly she said, "There is nothing I did that made my good readers good and there is nothing I can do to help my poor readers improve. If they can't read well by sixth grade, it's too late."

I knew from personal experience that she was wrong. I thought about my own journey as a reader. I didn't really learn how to read until I was in my thirties. If it hadn't been too late for me to become a good reader, it certainly wasn't too late for Courtney. Here's how it happened for me.

As part of a staff development program, I joined an adult book club. It was in this setting that I finally learned how to read. At first, I was intimidated. There were some really good readers in this group. For several months I watched them create meaning. I was afraid to join in the discussions. Instead I sat quietly, noticing how they wrestled with meaning. There was no one right answer. People argued their points of view passionately and shared places in the text that substantiated their thinking. They read aloud portions and shared connections they had made between their lives and the book. They asked questions and drew inferences. Their discussions were different from the ones I remembered in high school and college. Plot and symbolism became secondary. No one was quizzed on literary elements. For the first time, I was beginning to see how real readers made sense of text.

Fake reading wasn't allowed in this group. In order for me to participate, I needed to bring something to the discussion. Just reading words left me unprepared. I was enchanted with their thinking. Their ideas about the book were fascinating, but I was more interested in how they arrived at those ideas. I wanted to do it, too.

While leading the discussion on *Imagining Argentina* (Thornton 1987), Steph made connections between the book and her travels to South America. She talked about Argentina's unstable regimes and how the conditions described in the book were the result of the Perons' rule. I didn't know anything about Argentina, and listening to Steph's connections helped me create a framework on which to build a deeper understanding. Her thinking triggered responses from others. Julie asked questions about the death squads and wondered exactly who was abducting Argentineans from their homes. Ellin drew inferences as she helped Julie answer her own questions. Plot hadn't even been mentioned, but with each comment I understood the story better.

By the time our group read *Beloved* (Morrison 1987), I was comfortable enough to admit that I didn't really understand several parts of the book. I asked if the others could tell me how they figured out what was going on. Steph laughed and told me she wasn't sure what was going on in some of the parts either. "That's why we are reading this book together," she said. It finally dawned on me; these readers had not come to book club knowing all the answers. They were depending on one another to construct meaning. That night we each shared what was happening inside our head. Ellin explained that when she talked with others her comprehension got better. Joetta said she liked to revisit and rethink sections of the book after she heard other people's interpretations. Asking questions helped Steph. Julie visualized when she read. By the end of the night, we had all become better readers of *Beloved*.

Watching expert readers taught me how important my own reading is. If I am going to help students become better readers, it is crucial that I read myself. The strategies I use to make sense of the text are the very strategies I need to teach to not only struggling readers but also college-bound students as well (see Chapter 4).

Disarming the Defenses

People who read well often take for granted the real-world payoffs. Struggling readers seldom get to experience how great it feels to finish a book. Or how helpful it is to read and understand a chapter in a textbook. They don't know how much fun it can be to escape day-to-day life by jumping into a good read. By ninth grade, many students have been defeated by test scores, letter grades, and special groupings. Struggling readers are embarrassed by their labels and often perceive reading as drudgery. They avoid it at all costs. Reading has lost its purpose and pleasure.

As a teacher, my toughest challenge is getting reluctant readers to read. Sadly, many don't see the value of reading. It isn't worthy of their time. Favorable memories can serve as powerful reminder that authentic reading is pleasurable as well as purposeful. I trust that at some time in their lives, reading was gratifying. Early in the year, I am determined to help students rediscover at least one positive memory and use it as a cornerstone for future reading successes.

An activity I use to bring out the literacy histories of my students is the *important book and literary histories* form (see Figure 1.1). I ask students to recall a book that has had an impact on their life. It doesn't have to be a favorite book, but it does have to be an *important* one: one that leaves an impression. The memory can be positive or negative. If possible, the student brings the book to class. If the book is not available, students draw an illustration that resembles the cover. It is important for them to have something to hold on to as they stand in front of the class: it alleviates some of the stress speaking in front of their peers causes.

I model the activity by sharing a few important-book memories of my own. I bring in a basket filled with books that have shaped me as a reader, that represent years of learning to read.

I start with an early memory, one of being read to. I begin to recite, "Over in the meadow in the sand and the sun lived an old mother turtle and her little turtle one. Swim, said the mother." I change my voice to sound like a baby turtle. "I'll swim, said the little one." I notice a few girls with pink and orange hair rolling their eyes and muttering that this is going to be a long year. I continue in my mommy turtle voice, "So they swam all day in the sand and the sun."

"That poem," I announce with delight, "is from one of my all-time favorite books." Carefully, I pull the largest one from the basket and open the navy blue cloth cover. I gently glide my hands over the gold-embossed Humpty Dumpties scattered inside. I remember how this literature

---

Important Book and Literary Histories

Most everyone can remember a book that has had an impact on his or her life. Often this book is connected to a pleasurable experience. It could have been the first book you learned to read. It could have been a book that troubled you. An important book doesn't necessarily have to be well loved. Think about your history as a reader. Recall a book that sticks out in your mind and complete the following:

Title:
Author:
Give two reasons why the book is important to you:
1.
2.
Literary histories can often determine how we read and write. Past reading experiences influence our current reading and writing. List five positive or negative reading and/or writing events that affect the way you read and write today.
1.
2.
3.
4.
5.

Figure 1.1

anthology was kept high on a shelf, out of the reach of grimy little hands. "I've never actually read this book," I say, "but I know a lot of it by heart. When I was little, I made my mom read *Over in the Meadow* [Wadworth 1938] time and time again.

Melissa laughs. "I did that with *Goodnight Moon* [Brown 1947]. My mom got really sick of reading that book. Once she hid it, thinking I'd listen to another one. I threw a fit. Finally she gave in. I heard that book so many times, I knew it by heart." Her friends laugh as they begin to remember their personal favorites.

"In retrospect," I continue, "the best thing about this book wasn't the words, it was being alone with my mom. I would snuggle by her side as she read in her best read-aloud voice, poems and stories, tales about gingerbread boys and the raggedy man. Each day for a few precious minutes I had my mom all to myself. Those quiet moments were my first fond memories of learning how to read."

I reach into the basket for another book and pull out *The Wind in the Willows* (Grahame 1908). "I haven't read this book either, but I hate it." A few kids give me a funny look, surprised that a reading teacher would say such a thing. "Every fall I try to read it, and it brings back such bad memories I always abandon it after three or four chapters."

"Why?" Kandice asks.

"It all started with my friend Carol. She was reading *The Wind in the Willows,* and since she was reading it, I wanted to read it too. Carol was the prettiest girl in third grade. She had long brown hair with ends that always held a curl. Her bows matched her outfits, and in a fifty-yard dash she could beat any kid in the school, even the sixth-grade boys. Everyone wanted to be Carol's friend, and to prove it they did things they really didn't want to do. I chose a book that I really didn't want to read.

"We had to have our books approved. I remember walking up to the teacher's desk and thinking to myself that I was choosing a pretty thick book. I figured I'd be okay because Carol and I could read it together. The next minute, the teacher grabbed the book from my hands and said, 'You can't read this. It's way too hard for you. You aren't a good enough reader to read this book. Go choose an easier one.' I was so embarrassed. I told Carol I was going to read the same book she was and now I had to make up an excuse, explaining why I wasn't reading it."

"Teachers used to tell me that all the time," says Leigha. "It made me feel stupid. So I stopped trying to read challenging books all together."

"Yeah, I used to pick books to read just because my friends were reading them. It was dumb, because then I wouldn't even try to read. I'd just let them do all the work," confesses Rachel.

"I know what you mean," I agree. "I've done it too."

I continue sharing books and memories. There were Bronco Sundays at my grandparents. Waiting patiently for halftime when Grandpa would read the funnies aloud. I share important life lessons I have learned from *Yertle the Turtle* (Suess 1958) and *Robin Red Breast* (Hubbard 1959). I share how I burned myself reading under the covers with a flashlight trying to finish *Ramona the Pest* (Cleary 1968) without my father's knowing. I describe the time my husband and I read *The Autobiography of Malcolm X* (Haley 1964), racing to see who could finish first and arguing on the way as we changed our opinions about this man who caused such great controversy and change. I tell them how *The Old Man and the Sea* (Hemingway 1952) taught me about perseverance and that everyone has to read *Tuesdays with Morrie* (Albom 1997) before it's too late to change. Before I know it, forty-nine wonderful minutes have passed. The bell rings. Tomorrow it will be their turn to share.

The next day, Jerome volunteers to go first. He is by far the toughest kid I have ever taught. No one crosses Jerome. (As I write this, he is serving a life sentence for proving his gang allegiance by committing a drive-by shooting in which someone ended up dead.) When he asks to go first, I am nervous to say the least. Will he make a mockery out of the assignment? He hides his book behind his back and swaggers to the front of the room. Everyone waits breathlessly. I am dying to see what book he has. Slowly, he pulls it from behind his back. It is torn and tattered, obviously well loved. Jerome looks me in the eye and says, "My important book is ...*The Poky Little Puppy* [Lowrey 1942]." No one dares crack a smile, let alone chuckle. Jerome continues, "I loved this book. Every day after school when I was in first grade my grandma would teach me to read it. It was the first book I could read by myself." Jerome heads back to his seat. As he passes me, I notice a faint smile on his face. We have seen a side of Jerome that few have ever seen.

David, a football player who as a high school freshman already has the varsity coaches salivating because of his size, volunteers to go next. "My favorite book was a present from my kindergarten teacher, Mrs. King. On the last day of school, she gave us each a wrapped book." As an aside, he turns to me: "That must have taken her a long time to wrap all those books." He turns back to the class and continues: "Mrs. King told us to practice reading every day so when we got to first grade we would be good readers. I practiced all summer long. I didn't want to disappoint her." Carefully, David opens his beloved book and begins reading aloud. Just like a good elementary school teacher, he makes sure he holds the book so everyone can see the pictures. When he finishes, he returns to his seat, high-fiving students along the way.

As a class we will read powerful text. It will change our thinking forever. Our reading will compel us to share our pasts, passions, and concerns. Creating meaning together will force total strangers to connect. We will reveal strengths, expose our weaknesses, and grow stronger as we build a community of readers.

Books will be the great equalizer. Every student knows what it feels like to be a reading failure. They know what it's like to read a book and not "get it." They know how to fake-read and avoid real reading at all costs. I look around my classroom filled with reading failures. The important-book assignment reminds me that even these kids want to be good readers. I see the faces of my new students and know I must cross boundaries of race, religion, gender, and social status. I know this can be done only by sharing our experiences as readers because, after all, who can be intimidated by someone whose favorite book is *The Poky Little Puppy*.

The Realities of Reading

As a classroom teacher and literacy staff developer, I am often asked why so many middle and high school students are struggling to read well. I sense that the people who pose this question want a concise answer, a simple solution to a complex problem. There isn't one. In general, the public's perception of reading is simplistic. Many believe that reading is merely sounding out words. They don't stop to consider what sophisticated thought processes are involved and that reading becomes more demanding as students get older. Adolescents today are expected to plow through difficult material in a short time with little or no reading instruction.

Middle and high school teachers are required to cover vast amounts of material, so it is essential that students have the ability and the motivation to read on their own. More and more teachers are realizing that this is an unrealistic expectation. Granted there are secondary students who do choose to read and do it very well. However, if you are reading this book, it is probably because you have students who can read but choose not to or who try to read but have difficulty doing it.

Few middle and high school teachers feel they have the time or the expertise to teach students how to read. They have been trained in their content area and are uncomfortable stepping into the role of reading specialist. Consider for a moment a typical high school history teacher, who teaches five classes a day, each with between twenty-five and thirty students. His first two classes are U.S. history. The good news is, he only needs to worry about history involving the United States. The bad news is, he must begin with the Pre-Columbian Era and go all the way through with the present day.

This teacher also has two sections of world history. This course is divided into centuries, which means he must cover approximately 1,500 years, give or take a few decades, each semester. His last class is world geography. This is easy, unless of course there is a civil war somewhere in the world and a portion of land becomes a new country. In that case, he must revamp all of his course material from that part of the world.

Imagine the depth of information a history teacher must know in order to teach each of these classes. This expectation to cover an unbelievable amount of material is not uncommon. Often there is more information to be taught than there is time to teach it. Many teachers ask, "Even if I knew how to teach reading, when would I do it?"

Nevertheless, middle and high school teachers can and must teach students to be better readers of their course material. Critics argue, "If middle and high school students could read better, then more content could be covered. They could read at home and understand the information, and teachers could move through material faster." Right! Teachers would love this to be the case, but it isn't. Many students aren't reading at home, and they aren't understanding what they read in school. The material students encounter in secondary school is complicated and not understood by just "reading the words." It requires a variety of thinking processes, many of which need to be taught. Middle and high school students don't automatically know how to cope with rigorous reading material just because they've left elementary school.

By the time struggling readers reach sixth grade, many of them can "play the game." They disguise their reading weaknesses and "just get by." They complete their assignments but get little out of the material because they aren't able to use it.

The two types of struggling readers most often encountered in secondary schools are *resistive readers* and *word callers*. Resistive readers can read but choose not to. Word callers can decode the words but don't understand or remember what they've read.

I'll Do Anything but Read

When I think of resistive readers, I think of Lisa, a twelfth grader who has managed to avoid reading most of her high school career. Lisa is a fair student who plans to attend community college after graduation. She knows how to read but doesn't get much practice doing it. Lisa sometimes reads for pleasure, as long as she gets to pick the material. I've seen her read fashion magazines and compact disk inserts but that's about it. Lisa readily admits that she doesn't do school reading.

How can Lisa pass her courses without reading? I ask her how she does it. "It's easy," she says. "I sit in the back of the classroom and wait for one of the smart kids to answer the teacher's questions."

"What if no one knows the answer?" I ask.

"It doesn't matter," says Lisa. "If no one talks, the teacher gives us the answer."

I explain to Lisa and the rest of the class that teachers don't lecture just to hear themselves talk. They don't plan to recap every reading assignment so kids don't have to read. This takes away from valuable instructional time. But when students don't read or don't understand what they read, they get further and further behind, and the teacher feels obligated to help them catch up. Unfortunately, that sometimes means feeding them information.

A few days later I ask the class to read an essay and note what they think about it in the margins. The room is silent, and as I confer with a student here and there, I see everyone is busy. Or so I think. Chris is just a little too still. I stare at him. I can't tell whether he is sleeping or reading. His baseball cap is pulled down low on his forehead, and an elbow rests on the desk, the palm of that hand bracing the side of his cheek. Then I see the telltale bit of drool at the side of his mouth.

My chuckle wakes Chris up. I tell him how impressed I am with his ability to fake-read. Later he tells me it's too late for him to learn how to read well. He has made it through four years of high school without reading and he surely doesn't plan to start now. He has survived by listening to teachers recap what he was supposed to have read. I am saddened by his comment and wonder how he has slipped through the cracks.

Lisa and Chris have learned that if they are patient, the teacher will eventually feed them the information they need to know. Many resistive readers survive by listening to the teacher and copying the work of others. Students like Lisa and Chris, who can read but choose not to, soon lose the knack. When they need to take college entrance exams or complete a project at work, there won't be any smart kids shouting out answers or teachers feeding them what they need to know. They will be on their own and out of practice. Lectures and class discussions may help resistive readers cope temporarily, but sooner or later their lack of reading will catch up with them.

I Read the Words but What Do They Mean?

Word callers have mastered decoding and, as a bonus, also choose to read. However, they don't understand that reading involves thinking. They go through the motions of reading but assume all they have to do is pronounce words. When they don't understand or remember what they have read, they quit. Word callers are fairly good students but often don't do well with tasks that require them to use the words they read to think on their own. These readers feel powerless because the only strategy they have for gaining meaning is sounding out words.

Mike, an eleventh grader, marches into world literature one morning and announces to anyone who will listen that he read the assignment the night before but has no idea what he read. His frustration is apparent as he complains that he is sick of reading "stuff that doesn't make sense." Mike is a typical adolescent. His ability to understand difficult text is limited because he doesn't know how to go beyond the words. He has no reading strategies to help him construct meaning.

Tim, another eleventh grader, also struggles with difficult text. Like Mike he expects meaning to arrive immediately after he reads the words. He doesn't know good readers construct meaning. One day in class, Tim interrupts my lesson to accuse me of wasting everyone's time. He isn't interested in historical background knowledge.

Tim reminds me that I am teaching English, not history, and to please get on with the assignment so he can get started with his homework. I explain that when a reader has some background knowledge about a complicated piece of literature, he can make connections to it and understand it better. Tim doesn't care about background knowledge. In his opinion all he needs are the words. It hasn't occurred to him that decoding is not enough, that learning how to employ comprehension strategies will help him understand the words he reads.

Teachers of adolescents often encounter readers like Mike and Tim who expect to comprehend what they read by simply pronouncing the words. These students aren't concerned with understanding the material well. They want to complete the assignment so they can earn a grade. When reading the words alone doesn't produce meaning, word callers assume the material is too difficult and not worth the time it takes to master it. They may try sounding out the words, rereading portions of the text, or guessing at meaning. These strategies alone, however, aren't effective when trying to comprehend difficult text.

Tim spent the majority of the semester trying to change the way I taught. He loathed the fact that he could no longer breeze through a book without intellectual involvement. He didn't like it when I asked the class to think beyond the words, to interact with the author, and to use the information to draw conclusions. I was trying to reshape Tim's definition of reading, but he was comfortable with the one he had. It was easier to make his teachers responsible for his learning. He was used to sitting in class and being told what to think. He was comfortable parroting the comments of the teacher. When it came time for him to ask questions or make connections, Tim was stuck. He hated thinking on his own. He didn't want to be in charge of his own learning. When confusion set in, Tim thought it was the teacher's job to fix it.

Tim wasn't the only one of my students with this limited perception of reading. Many adolescents are comfortable being told what to think by teachers. I was trying to teach my students how to be better thinkers not just spit back facts. Students are used to being tested on what they understand. I was trying to teach them how to understand. Too many bright kids are wasting time sitting in back of the classroom expecting to be filled with knowledge. It's time to pull the plug on this type of behavior and begin teaching adolescents of all ages and reading abilities how to understand what they read so they can begin constructing meaning on their own.

Redefining Reading

Understanding how meaning is constructed from print is essential if teachers are to improve the comprehension of their students. Decoding is not comprehending. Certainly all good readers can recall a time when they were able to decode words but didn't understand what the words said. Maybe they were trying to read a legal document, like a lease or a tax form. Perhaps they were trying to understand a set of directions that looked and sounded like English but when it came to assembling the parts seemed more like Greek. Decoding is just the beginning. In order to construct meaning, readers also need to employ reading strategies.

Often parents will say to me, "My child is a good reader. He just has trouble with comprehension." What do these parents think reading is? It startles me when people define a child's reading level by his or her ability to decode words. Reading must be about thinking and constructing meaning. It's much more than pronouncing words. Researchers today define reading as a complex, recursive thinking process (Fielding and Pearson 1994; Ogle 1986). P. David Pearson and several of his colleagues have synthesized years of research on characteristics of proficient readers and isolated seven strategies used by successful readers of all ages (Pearson et al. 1992):

- They use existing knowledge to make sense of new information.
- They ask questions about the text before, during, and after reading.
- They draw inferences from the text.
- They monitor their comprehension.
- They use "fix-up" strategies when meaning breaks down.
- They determine what is important.
- They synthesize information to create new thinking.

Researchers Ellin Keene and Susan Zimmermann add creating sensory images to this list of comprehension strategies. In their book *Mosaic of Thought* (1997) they show how teachers can systematically teach thinking strategies to young children in order to help them better comprehend text. As the former project director of Public Education Business Coalition

(PEBC), Ellin Keene has guided the work of hundreds of Colorado teachers. Her work emphasizes the importance of teaching readers how to think.

In my classroom, above the chalkboard, are giant purple letters that say *Reading Is Thinking*. When readers construct meaning, they do so by way of deliberate, thoughtful cognition. They must do more than decode words. Decoding is important, but it is only one part of the process by which readers comprehend. They must also understand concepts and register subtleties. They need to determine what is important as well as connect their knowledge and experience to what they read.

Twenty-five years ago Rumelhart (1976) identified six *cueing systems* that readers use to understand text. The first three are *surface structures*, which are typically emphasized during the primary grades and provide the reader with visual and auditory clues for recognizing and pronouncing words as well as understanding sentence structure:

Graphophonic cues relate to letters, combinations of letters, and the sounds associated with them.

Lexical cues relate to words, including their instantaneous recognition, but not necessarily the meaning associated with them.

Syntactic cues relate to the form and structure of words and sentences that make up pieces of texts, including whether they "sound right" and are organized cohesively.

The remaining three cueing systems are *deep structures*. They allow the reader to interpret, analyze, and draw inferences from text. These cueing systems are rarely explicitly taught at the middle and secondary level, even though they are the means by which we understand difficult text.

Semantic cues relate to the meaning(s), concepts, and associations of words and longer pieces of text, including understanding subtle definitions and nuances.

Schematic cues relate to the reader's prior knowledge and/or personal experiences. They allow the reader to understand and remember what has been read. (These cues also group and organize new information in memory.)

Pragmatic cues relate to what the reader considers important and what he or she needs to understand for a particular purpose. They also include the social construction of meaning, in which groups of readers arrive at shared meaning and increasingly abstract interpretations. (PEBC 2000)

Colleen Buddy, a friend and colleague, compares these cueing systems to an orchestra: each section of instruments contributes to the sound of the symphony. When one or two sections stop playing, the quality of the music is diminished. The melody is still recognizable but it's not nearly as beautiful as when the whole orchestra is playing.

Cueing systems affect readers in much the same way. When all systems are operating, they are able to understand fully what they are reading. However, if one or two systems shut down, much of the meaning is lost. We may comprehend some of the piece, but we won't appreciate it completely. Successful readers know how to take advantage of all six cueing systems; struggling readers rely too heavily on one or two and miss a great deal of the text's richness. Readers who focus solely on surface structures decode words but don't remember what they've read. To observers, they seem to be good readers, and they themselves feel as though they are reading; but unless they construct meaning, they are not comprehending.

Teachers who are familiar with these cueing systems understand the complexities of reading and are therefore better able to help students learn to use all the cues available to them. Restrictive reading programs that prescribe one method of instruction or emphasize only one or two cueing systems can't meet the needs of every student. Dogmatic reading philosophies promote inflexibility and force teachers to teach the prescribed programs rather than the child.

Shouldn't They Have Learned This in Elementary School?

Sometimes teacher expectations interfere with instruction. A high school student teacher asked me, "Why do I have to teach reading? Shouldn't students learn how to read in elementary school?" Before I could respond with the platitude that it is everyone's responsibility to teach students how to read, she threw out another question: "Do you realize only eight of my twenty-two students can read the science textbook?"

I told her her second question had answered her first. Standing in front of twenty-two students and assigning them inaccessible material they can't read is a waste of time. Text becomes inaccessible when students:

1. *Don't have the comprehension strategies necessary to unlock meaning.* Students who have only one or two strategies for making meaning struggle to understand difficult text.

2. *Don't have sufficient background knowledge.* Students who don't already know something about what they are reading can't make connections. What they read seems disconnected and unimportant.

3. *Don't recognize organizational patterns.* Students who don't understand how text is organized usually don't know what is important. They can't

prioritize and therefore don't establish a cognitive framework. They have no way to organize and store their thinking.

4. *Lack purpose.* Students who don't have a purpose when they read usually lose interest in what they are reading and fail to construct meaning. It's hard to glean anything from the text when you don't know why you're reading it.

It's not that children haven't been taught to read in elementary school. Elementary teachers work hard trying to teach every child to read well. Rather, reading instruction needs to continue after elementary school. Reading instruction at the primary level focuses on decoding and reading with fluency. Intermediate instruction emphasizes meaning and ideas in both literature and nonfiction. Students begin to learn that reading should make sense.

However, many middle and secondary teachers assume that successful students are also strategic readers; therefore they don't spend much time teaching students how to read. They expect them:

- To know how to read.
- To read faster than they did in elementary school.
- To read large amounts of text in short amounts of time.
- To gain information by reading.
- To read and understand increasingly difficult material.

Reading requirements increase dramatically for adolescents. They are expected to be sophisticated readers, to use deep structures as well as surface structures. Secondary teachers focus on content. Unknown words are taught through vocabulary lessons and students are expected to learn about unfamiliar topics by reading nonfiction. Meanwhile, reading instruction continues to decline, at a time when it is needed most.

Teachers who struggle with the idea of teaching reading strategies, take heart! You don't need a master's degree in reading to help students become better readers. You can improve your students' comprehension by following just two suggestions:

1. *Become a passionate reader of what you teach.* After I had finished a demonstration lesson with a group of high school students, I overheard one teacher say to another, "Sure, those kids were willing to read what Cris gave them. It was interesting. I'd like to see her do that with the material my students have to read." I guarantee that if you don't like the material you're assigning, your students won't either. Search for interesting text and get it into the hands of your students. Rediscover

why you fell in love with the subject you teach and why you wanted to teach it to others. Take time to read. Weed out the dull, poorly written text. Give your students the gift of something wonderful to read.

2. *Model how good readers read.* Think about what you as a reader do to construct meaning and share this information with your students. Different types of reading require different strategies. Don't feel pressured to teach all your students how to read everything well. Just show them how you read the material you assign.

What's to Come?

As you read this book, you will quickly notice that it isn't a comprehensive work about reading instruction. It isn't intended to be. There are no prescribed activities that are part of a definitive way to teach reading.

Each chapter begins with a student quote and an anecdote illustrating a problem I've faced in my own classroom. (You may recognize similar problems in your own classroom.) I explain how I address the dilemma, focusing on what good readers do to make sense of text. At the end of each chapter there is a section, headed What Works, that gives simple suggestions that teachers can use to make their content more accessible.

As you read this book, rethink your instructional role. Examine your current teaching methods and avoid pressures to cover content. Try to sidestep the temptation to feed your students information. Don't reduce the opportunities your students have to read because they are having difficulty. Teach them the strategies that will help them read the assigned material, and assign interesting, accessible text. Be confident that, yes, you do know something about teaching reading. The very fact that you can read makes you something of an expert.

Part 2

IN SUPPORT OF STRATEGIC READING

Purposes for Reading: Access Tools

I read everything the same way. It doesn't matter if it is my science book or *Sports Illustrated*. What's the point? Reading is reading.

Luke, grade 10

"How many of you buy compact disks?" I ask the class during reading workshop. Everyone in the room raises a hand. "How many of you pull out the CD insert when you put the CD on for the first time?" Once again everyone raises a hand. "Why do you do that?"

Kellie giggles. "I want to see what the band members look like."

"I'm looking for the words to the songs," smiles Stephanie.

"I wonder if there are drawings or hidden pictures with secret meanings," confesses Chris.

I point out that each one of them has a purpose for looking through the insert. I want students to understand that good readers have purposes other than pleasure for their reading. To reinforce the point, I ask, "How many of you read the sports page?" Many boys who claim to hate reading raise their hand. "Why do you read the sports page, Tony?" I ask.

"I read it to see how other basketball teams are doing," he says.

"I read it to find out about players I like," says Josh.

Brian adds that he reads to get scores and statistics.

I ask the boys how knowing what they are looking for helps them.

"It helps me save time," says Tony.

"Right. It helps you locate information more quickly. You don't waste time reading parts you aren't interested in," I elaborate. "How else does establishing a purpose help you?"

"It helps me decide what to skip and what to read," says Butch.

"Good point," I say. "Having a purpose helps readers determine what is important."

Purpose Is Everything

A reader's purpose affects everything about reading. It determines what's important in the text, what is remembered, and what comprehension strategy a reader uses to enhance meaning. When students read difficult text without a purpose, they express the following complaints:

- I don't care about the topic.
- I can't relate to the topic.
- I daydream and my mind wanders.
- I can't stay focused.
- I just say the words so I can be done.
- I get bored.

Readers behave like this when they don't have a reason for reading. They pronounce the words, finish the assignment, and rarely come away with a thorough understanding. It is a waste of time; they haven't constructed meaning and can't use the information.

According to researchers Pichert and Anderson (1977), readers determine what is important based on their purpose for reading. When I ask students why they read outside of school, they usually have a reason—but they don't think it counts, because it isn't school related. When I ask students why they read in school, they say their teacher makes them: "Read chapter 10. There will be a test on Monday." Or, "Finish reading acts 1 and 2 so you can write a character analysis." Rarely do students have the opportunity to determine their own purpose for reading. It is no wonder they come to rely solely on the teacher for the reasons they read.

Unfortunately the teacher's purpose is often too vague to help. Her psychology teacher told Michelle, an excellent student, that there would be a test on the first three chapters in the textbook. When Michelle asked for more specifics, the teacher reiterated, "Just read and know the information in the first three chapters." Michelle knew she couldn't remember that much material and didn't know how to determine what was important.

Michelle isn't an exception. Most students don't know how to set their own purpose. They tend to think everything they read in a textbook is equally important. As I prepared for my first biology exam as a college freshman, I diligently highlighted anything and everything that seemed remotely important. After all, this was college, and I was reading a college textbook. I felt I needed to memorize the text, and I thought highlighting the majority of it would do the trick. My purpose was too broad. It didn't allow me to distinguish main ideas from interesting details.

I could have highlighted places in the text that were confusing, but that still would have been much too broad a purpose. I didn't have enough background knowledge to understand most of what I was reading. A better purpose would have been to find places in the text that were connected to the class lectures. That would have helped me determine what the professor thought was important and therefore what might be on the test.

Students need to be taught why it is important to have purpose and how to establish one. The following passage, from Pichert and Anderson (1977), is a wonderful example to use to demonstrate why it is important to set a purpose.

The House

The two boys ran until they came to the driveway. "See, I told you today was good for skipping school," said Mark. "Mom is never home on Thursday," he added. Tall hedges hid the house from the road so the pair strolled across the finely landscaped yard. "I never knew your place was so big," said Pete. "Yeah, but it's nicer now than it used to be since Dad had the new stone siding put on and added the fireplace."

There were front and back doors and a side door which led to the garage which was empty except for three parked 10-speed bikes. They went in the side door, Mark explaining that it was always open in case his younger sisters got home earlier than their mother.

Pete wanted to see the house so Mark started with the living room. It, like the rest of the downstairs, was newly painted. Mark turned on the stereo, the noise of which worried Pete. "Don't worry, the nearest house is a quarter mile away," Mark shouted. Pete felt more comfortable observing that no houses could be seen in any direction beyond the huge yard.

The dining room, with all the china, silver, and cut glass, was no place to play so the boys moved into the kitchen where they made sandwiches. Mark said they wouldn't go to the basement because it had been damp and musty ever since the new plumbing had been installed.

"This is where my Dad keeps his famous paintings and his coin collection," Mark said as they peered into the den. Mark bragged that he could get spending money whenever he needed it since he'd discovered that his Dad kept a lot in the desk drawer.

There were three upstairs bedrooms. Mark showed Pete his mother's closet which was filled with furs and the locked box which held her jewels. His sisters' room was uninteresting except for the color TV which Mark carried to his room. Mark bragged that the bathroom in the hall was his since one had been added to his sisters' room for their use. The big highlight in his room, though, was a leak in the ceiling where the old roof had finally rotted.

Hand out a copy of these paragraphs to every student. Then:

1. Ask students to read the piece and circle with their pencil whatever they think is important. (In the five years I have used this piece, I have never once had a student ask me what he or she should circle. They all dive in seeming to know what to highlight.) When I do this activity with teachers, they usually set a purpose for themselves. They highlight the boys skipping school and often ask about the leaky ceiling in the bedroom.

2. Ask students to read the piece again and this time use a pink highlighter to mark places in the text a robber would find important. Students will notice that having a purpose makes it much easier to highlight important points.

3. Have the students read the piece a third time. Ask them to mark with a yellow highlighter any places in the story that a prospective home buyer might think are important. By now, it will be obvious how much easier it is to determine what is important when the reader has a purpose.

4. Ask students what they notice about the three times they highlighted. Point out that the first time was probably the hardest, because they didn't have a purpose.

5. On a projected transparency, jot down what students think is important for the robber and for the home buyer. Compare the two lists and discuss why each item is important. If an item is on both lists, discuss why both a robber and a home buyer would find it important.

Once students see the importance of establishing a purpose when they read, it's time to teach them different purposes for reading. Access tools are specific materials and strategies that help students organize and synthesize their thoughts as they read. They make material more accessible. Students of all grade levels can use these tools with almost any type of material. They'll quickly figure out which tool works best for their particular purpose.

Thinking Aloud

Thinking aloud shows students how an expert reader makes sense of text (Whimby 1975). By sharing your thinking out loud, you make the elusive process of comprehension more concrete.

During the mid-1980s Pearson, Roeller, Dole, and Duffy (1992) explored the merits of "mental modeling," or thinking out loud. Elementary teachers already knew how important it was for students to see them modeling the physical aspects of reading. Teachers no longer corrected papers or balanced their checkbook during sustained silent reading. They sat where everyone could see them and read right along with the students.

Some reading experts even suggested that teachers should occasionally laugh out loud or make a comment in response to the book so students could see a reader interacting with the text. I knew one teacher who actually staged responses for her students. As they barreled into the room after recess, for example, she would hold up her hand and implore them to be quiet for one more minute so she could finish the chapter.

Mental modeling is an even better way to help students understand how good readers comprehend text. When teachers make invisible mental processes visible, they arm young readers with powerful weapons. Good readers engage in mental processes before, during, and after they read in order to comprehend text. I stop often to think out loud for my students. I describe what is going on in my mind as I read. When I get stuck, I demonstrate out loud the comprehension strategies I use to construct meaning.

Thinking aloud for your students in this way is easy to do, requires little planning, and doesn't need to be graded. Here's how to go about it:

1. *Select a short piece of text.* It can be the first page of a novel or a difficult section of a textbook. Use what you think will be most appropriate for the mental process you wish to demonstrate. Whenever possible, make copies of the passage to give to students so they can follow along. I project a transparency of the text so that I can point to the words as I read.

2. *Foresee difficulty.* Consider what about the text might cause students to lose their way. Anticipate obstacles having to do with content, structure, or comprehension strategies. Figure out how you would tackle the problem. (Make sure not to overwhelm students with too many suggestions.)

   For example, if I want students to draw on their background knowledge, I would verbalize any information I have about the piece before I began reading. I would consider how the piece is organized, who the author is, and what I already know about the topic. With poetry, I would read the title first and use it to predict what the poem will be about. I would check to see whether I know who the poet is. If I do, I would explore what I know about his or her writing style.

   Content dictates which strategies to model. Background knowledge can be applied to any text. Mysteries require the reader to infer. Charts and graphs must be integrated with text. A social studies teacher may use the first paragraph of an assigned chapter to demonstrate the importance of asking questions while reading. A math teacher might

connect information taught in Chapter 11 to new information encountered in Chapter 12. It's up to you, the expert, the teacher, to decide
what to model.

3. *Read the text out loud and stop often to share your thinking.* Tell your students explicitly what you are doing: "Good readers use their background knowledge when they read. They think about what they know
before they begin reading." Remember, you read better than anyone
else in the room. Capture what you do as a good reader and communicate that to your students. When I am reading I make sure I am looking
at the words on the transparency. When I stop reading to think out
loud, I look at the students and share what is taking place inside my
head. Looking at the transparency when I read and looking at the students when I share thinking helps them distinguish the difference
between reading aloud and thinking aloud. (Although it is scary, occasionally reading a piece of text cold will give students an authentic
view of what a good reader does to make sense of text. Lots of students
think good readers make sense of everything they read the first time.)

4. *Point out the words in the text that trigger your thinking.* Be explicit in
how you get the meaning you do. Here are some examples:

When I read [words from the text], I am reminded of _____.
Good readers connect new knowledge to known information.

When I read [words from the text], I wonder _____. Good readers ask questions when they read in order to help themselves make
inferences.

I am confused when I read [words from the text], so I am going to
[specify the strategy you are using to try to clear up the confusion] to
get unstuck. Good readers recognize confusion and know how to
repair meaning when confusion sets in.

I notice that this piece is organized like this: [specify]. I am going to
use [a particular element of this structure] to help me understand the
text. Good readers look for organizational patterns in the text. It helps
them predict.

Thinking aloud in front of students takes away some of the comprehension guesswork they encounter. As you describe your thinking clearly,
students can see how a good reader makes meaning out of difficult text.
Once you've demonstrated thinking aloud a time or two, your students
can begin doing so in class. According to Silven and Vauras (1992) students who were encouraged to think aloud about what was happening in
their head as they read were better able to summarize information.
Meichebaum and Asnarow (1979) theorize that students who are asked to

think out loud are less impulsive about jumping to conclusions and seem more thoughtful and strategic about their reading. However, I would caution you not to turn the role of thinking aloud over to your students too quickly. First make sure your students "see" the wide range of possible thinking strategies they can use when they read.

Marking Text

You may be familiar with an instructional strategy called coding the text (Davey 1983). I have expanded this strategy to include sticky notes and highlighting.

I teach my students how to mark text early in the semester, because it gives them a way to stay engaged in their reading. Often students complain that they get sleepy or their mind wanders when they read. Marking text helps readers pay attention and remember what they read. Here's how it works:

1. Assign codes to the types of thinking in which you would like students to engage. Then, as students read, they are to mark these codes next to the passages in the text that trigger these kinds of thinking and explain the connection. For example:

   BK denotes connections the reader makes between her life and the text. Written responses can begin, "This reminds me of...."

   ? denotes questions the reader has about the text. Written responses can begin, "I wonder...."

   I denotes an inference or a conclusion the reader draws from the text. Written responses can begin, "I think...."

2. Model the coding process for your students by thinking it through out loud. I mark the codes next to passages on a projected transparency and verbalize the mental process I am using. If I am teaching students how to use the BK code, I explain, very precisely, the connections I make between the text and my background knowledge and share how these connections help me understand the text better.

3. Give students accessible pieces to mark on their own—something within reach. If the text is too hard, students won't be able to practice the strategy. Make sure students not only mark the text with the code but also describe their thinking. Encourage all serious attempts.

   Be careful not to assign too many codes at once. I recommend you begin with only one. When students are comfortable using the first code, add a second, and so on.

What if your students aren't allowed to write in their texts? Many times, books are the property of the school. You could photocopy portions of the text, but this can become expensive and you may be violating the copyright laws. A more reasonable solution is to write both the codes and the connection on a sticky note and attach it at the appropriate spot. (After all, this is how we often take notes in real life.)

4. Using highlighters. When my students encounter passages in the text they don't understand or ideas that need to be clarified, they highlight the text in yellow. Sometimes it is a word, sometimes an entire paragraph. Next to the highlighted portion, they write a fix-up strategy they tried in order to clear up their confusion.

Sometimes students don't know when they are confused, so they highlight nothing and claim to understand everything. Then I introduce pink highlighters as the way to help students distinguish what they understand from what they find confusing.

I select a short piece of text and tell students they have to highlight every word on the page, either in yellow or in pink. This forces them to decide what they understand and what they don't. (They must be able to explain anything they mark in pink to a classmate.) Use this activity sparingly. It becomes tedious if used too often.

Using Double-Entry Diaries

Double-entry diaries (DEDs) are similar to the Cornell method of taking notes—dividing a page in half with questions and main ideas on the left and specific information on the right. However, a DED is more flexible and can be used in a multitude of ways. You get to choose how you want students to structure their thinking, while students get to show you what they are thinking. Here's how I do it:

1. Students divide a piece of notebook paper in half lengthwise, "like a hot-dog bun."

2. In the left-hand column, students copy sentences or words directly from the text. (They can also summarize the passage.) If more than one page is involved, they should include the page number so you can find the quotation if you need to.

3. In the right-hand column of the page, students write down their inferential and critical thinking about the word, sentences, or summary they wrote on the left-hand side.

Here is an example:

Direct quote from text and page number	**Thinking options**
	This reminds me of
	or
	I wonder
	or
	I infer
	or
	This is important because
	or
	I am confused because
	or
	I will help myself by
	or
	The picture in my head looks like
	or
	I think this means

I recommend you begin by selecting one thinking option from the right-hand side. If students are given all the above choices, they become overwhelmed and distracted. Start off slowly and model whatever thinking option you want students to use.

If I want students to make connections between what they've read earlier in the semester to what they are reading now, I might choose "This reminds me of." With a transparency ready on which to write my quotations and my thinking, I begin reading a selection aloud. Occasionally, I stop to pull a quote from the book. I copy the words from the text on the left-hand side of the transparency, and on the right-hand side share how the quote is connected to my personal knowledge or experience. Sometimes a single word will ignite a connection. Other times, it is an entire sentence or paragraph.

Double-entry diaries can be constructed in a variety of ways, but the essence is always the same: the left-hand side (a quote or a summary) is lifted directly from the text; the right-hand side is the reader's reaction to the words copied from the text. Below are some examples of DEDs I have used with science, social studies, and math classes:

List interesting facts or details	What is the author's message?
Confusing part in text	What I did to try to get unstuck
Term/vocabulary word causing confusion	What I know about the term/confusion

The appendix contains samples of several DEDs that can be adapted to specific instructional needs. DEDs give students an opportunity to share their thinking. They can ask questions, identify confusion, and make connections to content. They can begin to construct meaning by interacting with some aspect of the text.

Using Comprehension Constructors

A *comprehension constructor* often requires readers to use two or more thinking strategies and is typically introduced after students know how to mark text and use a double-entry diary. Essentially, it's a worksheet you design to guide your students through difficult text using a particular comprehension strategy. (I grade mine for both effort and completeness.)

The comprehension constructor below is one I've used to help students make inferences while reading Tim O'Brien's (1969) "Man at the Well":

1. Call up any background knowledge you have about war, Vietnam, and elderly people.

2. Read "Man at the Well."

3. As you read the piece, you should have a number of questions. Jot them down in the margins where they occur to you. (I want to see at least three.)

4. At the end of the piece, write a response. It should be a paragraph of at least four sentences.

5. Look back at the questions you asked. Write the three best questions below and then decide where the answers to the questions can be found: in the text, in your head, in another source. (Raphael et al. 1986)
   A)
   B)
   C)

In this comprehension constructor I'm trying to get my students to make inferences. In order to draw an inference, you have to use your background knowledge and question the text. If you aren't curious and don't have any questions about a piece, it is difficult to draw a complex inference. Notice I am more concerned with students' thinking processes than I am with right answers.

Here's how to go about designing a comprehension constructor:

1. Anticipate difficulties students may encounter in a particular text. Ask yourself how you would address each difficulty. Would you make a

connection to background knowledge? Would you ask a question and try to answer the question by drawing a conclusion?

2. Decide what comprehension strategies you would like students to use. Design steps that will guide students through the same processes you used to understand the piece.

Accept the fact that you may have to revise the comprehension constructor if you find it doesn't address the strategy in the way you hoped it would. Focus on process. If students concentrate on the way they think about what they read, they will be more likely to understand it. (The appendix contains more examples of comprehension constructors.)

The Importance of Modeling

When teaching your students how to access text, make sure to model how a particular tool is used. In the beginning, choose a text that is not too difficult. Point out how the access tool allows you to hold on to your thinking so you can remember and use what you've read later. When you ask students to use an access tool themselves, give them feedback. Once students are more comfortable with the tool, have them use it on more challenging pieces of text. Encourage students to use the tools outside of the classroom. Help them see the practicality of each tool, how it makes difficult text more accessible.

Access tools help you make text understandable without spending hours of class time teaching reading. They encourage students to participate in their reading instead of relying on you to deliver the information. They help readers negotiate text so they can remember and use what they have read. When readers know how to use these tools, they naturally determine purposes and become more engaged in their reading. Access tools make it possible for you to help students become better readers of the required material.

Then, the next time you ask your class to participate in a discussion, thirty pairs of eyes won't drop to the floor. Instead, students will gladly share their thinking.

■ ■ ■ ■ ■ ■ *What Works*

1. Share real-world reasons for reading and why it is important to set a purpose. Keep track of everything you read for one day. Record everything from a heady novel to the daily newspaper. Demonstrate how you

determine what is important in text and what isn't. Think of all the material that gets put into your mailbox at school. Some of it is important, some isn't. Share how you decide what to read. Point out how your purpose determines what you remember. You will probably surprise yourself how much reading you do. It all counts.

TEACHING POINT: Good readers read for different purposes. Having a purpose helps readers remember what they read and helps them determine what is important.

2. Watch yourself make meaning when you read. Notice what you and other good readers do to make sense. Join a book club and pay attention to your thinking as you read. Talk to others about how they make sense of the text. Most people will want to tell you *what* they read. Steer them back to the process of *how they made sense* of the text by asking what they did to make meaning.

TEACHING POINT: Good readers know that in order to understand what they read, they must do more than pronounce words. They understand that if comprehension is to occur, they must engage in several thinking processes. Good readers are aware of their thinking.

3. Experiment with using access tools in your own reading. Try marking text or using a double-entry diary. Notice how it helps you hold on to your thinking. Readers want to remember what they have read so they can use the information later. Show students how access tools can help them hold on to their thinking too.

TEACHING POINT: Good readers don't remember everything they read. They use tools to hold on to their thinking so they can return to it later. Access tools allow readers to use the text to justify and support their thinking.

4. Model your thinking as you read in front of your students. Share everything from confusing text and how you repair meaning to text that moves you emotionally. Let students see all the different ways a reader can bring meaning to text. Let students in on what real readers do. Read professional material as well as leisure material; allow students to see reading as a lifelong and life-enhancing activity.

TEACHING POINT: Good readers are flexible in their thinking and use different strategies for different types of reading. Good readers perceive reading as something they will do for their entire life, not just to pass a class.

Conversations with Cantos: Tracking Confusion to Its Source

My inner voice talks to me when I need help. It guides me, telling me when I am confused. It forces me to ask questions about the book and my life. It helps me understand what I am reading.

T.J., grade 12

One day a struggling tenth grader named Dan changes my teaching forever. In a rather irritated voice he says, "I'm sick and tired of you telling the class that it's our job to know when we know and know when we don't know. You're the teacher. Aren't you the one who is supposed to know when we understand something and when we don't?"

Astonished, I ask him to clarify what he means.

"That's what teachers get paid for, isn't it? How am I supposed to know when I don't get something? I'm just a kid."

"Actually, Dan," I answer, "you're asking me to be a mind reader, and no, teachers don't get paid for that. Think about it. If you don't even know when you are stuck, how am I supposed to know?"

For too long, teachers have been expected to monitor every aspect of their students' comprehension. We do our best to assess understanding, but expecting us to monitor everyone's comprehension, in every instance, is expecting the impossible. When we assume the sole responsibility for monitoring comprehension, our students gladly relinquish control over their reading. Dan misunderstands my job and the reader's role. He doesn't know he is supposed to be the one in charge of his reading and that it is his job to be conscious of the thinking taking place inside his head. Dan is the only one who can truly know when he understands something. He has to learn how to help himself when he becomes confused.

When Dan announced that it was my job to know when he was confused, I was shocked, then amused. Eventually, I realized the serious implications of his comment. Did everyone in the class expect me to be a mind reader? Had all the students abdicated their responsibility for understanding what they read? I had to find out what they knew about monitoring their comprehension.

The next day, I wrote two questions on the chalkboard at the beginning of class and asked my students to answer them the best they could:

- How do you know when you are confused?
- What do you do when you are confused?

Their responses made it clear that they didn't recognize confusion until they had to do something with the information, like answer questions or write a summary. Not until they tried to remember what they had read did they realize they weren't comprehending. When they couldn't remember what they read, they realized they were stuck. These readers weren't thinking about the processes occurring inside their head as they read. Most of them focused on decoding the words, not on thinking about what those words meant.

They rarely stopped while reading a piece to try to repair their confusion. They kept doggedly on until they finished the "assignment," even though they had no idea what they were reading. A few said they just hoped the confusion would go away. Some said they asked the teacher or someone else in the class for help.

Sadly, many of my students don't expect to understand what they read. They accept their confusion and figure that at this point in their life, it's too late for them to become better readers. They wait to be told what it is they have read. If no one does that, they just don't get it.

My first step is always to help these readers understand it's their job to comprehend what they read, not mine. Showing them how to monitor their thinking as they read helps them regain their confidence and puts them back in control of their reading.

Real-World Monitoring

I learned about monitoring my thinking from my father, who believes that baseball is a thinking man's sport. I remember hundreds of dinner table conversations, rehashing one of my brothers' performances on the baseball diamond. Nothing infuriated my father more than mental errors.

He expected the boys to think at all times when they were playing ball. He wanted them to analyze the pitchers so they could adjust their swing and know where to stand in the batter's box. He wanted them to plan where to throw the ball when they were fielding so they could react in an instant. He expected them to figure out why they got a good hit and why they struck out. He'd say, "The flight of the ball is directly related to the swing of the bat; only the batter can control how he hits the ball." If one of the boys was in a hitting slump, he'd ask him to think about his swing. "You popped the ball up three times to the third baseman. Why do you think that happened?" he'd ask. "Did you swing late? Were you opening up your hips too soon? Did you notice the pitcher in the first three innings was a lefty?" Likewise, when someone went four for four, he'd ask, "What did you do tonight that allowed you to hit the ball so well? Did you step toward the mound instead of away from it? Did you use a different bat?"

My father taught us to think not just about baseball but about every aspect of our lives. He asked questions that caused us to reflect. He modeled different ways of handling a situation so the next time it arose we'd know what to do. Most important, he wanted us to know how to help ourselves so we wouldn't become dependent on others. He knew the importance of teaching us how to monitor our thinking. He showed us examples of professional athletes, business people, and yes, even little leaguers who weren't aware of their thinking. They made the same mistakes over and over again because they weren't conscious of what they were doing. Likewise, he pointed out people who were cognizant of their thinking and how much better they were at work or play because they knew how to help themselves when they struggled. My father knew that if we recognized what we were doing when we were successful, we could re-create it when we weren't.

"I can't go up to the plate with you," my father said once. "When you're up there, you're all alone. It's your job to figure out how to get on base." Adolescents are often all alone when they are asked to read for school. They have to be able to recognize confusion so they can repair whatever has caused meaning to break down. If students aren't aware of their thinking, they make the same mistakes over and over again. Like anyone else, readers who are successful need to know when they are stuck so they can help themselves get unstuck. Readers who understand what they comprehend aren't wasting their time; when they finish reading, they are able to use the information.

How Do I Know I'm Stuck?

Once students acknowledge that they can and should be in control of their reading, they need to know when they are confused. There are indicators that help readers know when confusion or mind wandering is setting in. Many students don't recognize they are confused until it is too late. If students can recognize signals that indicate confusion, they can stop temporarily and decide how to help themselves. When Dan asked how he was supposed to know when he was stuck, he was really asking how he could identify his confusion.

There are six signals I teach my students to look for when they read:

1. The voice inside the reader's head isn't interacting with the text. Readers have two types of voices in their head as they read. One is them reciting the text. The other has a conversation with the text, in a sense talking back to the words on the page. Sometimes it asks questions. It can agree or disagree with the content. This voice interacts with the ideas on the page. When readers only hear themselves saying the words, they are confused or bored and won't remember what they have read.

2. The camera inside the reader's head shuts off. Good readers have a video camera playing inside their head as they read. When the camera shuts off and the reader can no longer get a visual image from the words, it is an indication that meaning has been interrupted.

3. The reader's mind begins to wander. Good readers catch themselves when they are thinking about something unrelated to the text. Thinking about something far removed from the material is a signal that readers must reconnect with their reading.

4. The reader can't remember what has been read. Good readers can usually retell some part of what they have read. If they can't remember anything at all, it is a signal they need to go back and repair meaning.

5. Clarifying questions asked by the reader are not answered. Good readers ask literal questions to clarify meaning. When these questions don't get answered, it is an indication that the reader needs more background knowledge or is not focused on the text.

6. The reader reencounters a character and has no recollection when that character was introduced. Good readers keep track of characters and know who they are. When a reader reencounters a character and has no recollection who that character is, it is a signal that the reader wasn't paying attention and needs to repair something that has caused meaning to break down.

Now That I Know I'm Stuck, What Do I Do?

Once readers recognize they are confused, they can begin helping themselves toward understanding. Any reader benefits when she or he recognizes signals of confusion. Students who take college preparatory classes are expected to read many difficult pieces and are often just as guilty as remedial readers when it comes to stopping and repairing breakdowns in meaning. Readers of all abilities need to know what to do when meaning is interrupted.

One year I had my world literature class tackle Dante's *Divine Comedy*. After we had read the majority of the long poem in class, I assigned six pages for them to read at home and asked them to focus on plot. I warned them there would be a quiz the following day, consisting of one question: "What happened in canto 34?" The class assured me this would be no problem. The bell rang and they left, confident they'd do well on the quiz.

The next morning, students filed into the room with panic-stricken faces, spouting excuses and whining that they didn't "get it." I leaned against the chalkboard and watched. Students flipped through their literature anthology as if frantic page turning would help them understand plot. "Just give me the F now," Rachel announced. "I read it but I have no idea what happened."

Students knew the quiz question and still they struggled. I hypothesized they didn't understand what they read because they were focusing only on the words and not the meaning. They weren't monitoring their comprehension. They had blasted through the words expecting meaning to arrive. Instead of stopping to figure out how to help themselves, they just kept reading.

Students swore up and down they did the assignment but just didn't understand what they read. I believed them. For the most part, these were A and B students who planned to attend college. They certainly didn't want a C or worse scarring their transcript. They were grade driven and, unlike many of my reading workshop students, did their homework and studied for tests. Surprisingly, these presumably good readers were as helpless as the remedial readers in reading workshop when challenged with difficult text.

I knew it would be pointless to give a quiz, let alone have a class discussion. Since I couldn't continue with my original lesson plans, my only alternative seemed to be to lecture for the rest of the period. Then I had a brainstorm. I could forgo the lecture that I knew few would listen to anyway and spend the time teaching a reading strategy that would help them understand the next part of the *Divine Comedy*. I had a decision to make: teach the reading or the reader? I chose to teach the reader, trusting that if I focused on process content would emerge.

I changed the format of the quiz and passed out yellow sticky notes to everyone in the room. I explained that since they didn't understand what happened in canto 34, now was the perfect time to teach them something about reading comprehension.

"Good readers know when they are confused and they do something to help themselves get unstuck. How many of you knew you were confused last night?" Most students raised a hand. "Terrific, all of you with your hand up should get an A+ on this quiz." The surprised hand raisers smirked at the know-it-alls who had pretended to understand everything.

Having asked the class to recognize their confusion, I knew we would now need to discuss content. I asked my students to find the place in the text where they first became confused, paste the sticky note there, and then describe their confusion on the sticky note.

"Great," Mike said sarcastically. "I'm stuck on the whole thing."

"That's okay," I told him. "Go back to the place where it first became confusing and mark that."

"I can't," whined Mike. "I'm stuck on the whole thing." The class laughed and several students slapped Mike a high five.

"Well, then I guess you fail the quiz." I'd recaptured Mike's attention.

"I flunk just because I don't know what I read?"

I explained that this quiz grade was based on their ability to identify their confusion. If they had understood everything they'd read, they could take the original quiz and summarize canto 34. If they couldn't explain what happened, they must have had some difficulty. Their option was to identify it. All they had to do to get credit was find a confusing part, mark it, and describe what they didn't understand or why they lost meaning. Blank sticky notes would earn no points.

"But I don't understand any of it," Mike grumbled again.

"Fine," I answered. "Go to the beginning of the canto and find the place where you started to become confused. Surely you understood some of the canto. Start with what you know. As you reread be conscious of your thinking and listen to that little voice in your head that says, 'I don't get this part.'"

"Pick anything we don't get?" asked Liana.

"Yes, but be ready to explain why you don't get it."

"Can it be a word we don't know?" Chris asked.

"Sure, it can be an unfamiliar word, or maybe it's a reference to a historic figure that you don't know. There is a lot of that in this canto. It may even be that your mind wandered and you caught yourself thinking about something unrelated to the reading."

To get them started, I shared a place in the text where I got confused, modeling my thinking out loud and writing on the board what I would write on the sticky note.

While students worked, I circulated through the room. Liana didn't know who the Roman poet Virgil was. Justine was stuck on a word. The class spent fifteen minutes working before I asked them to stop and share what they had written. They were eager to share their confusions. Even Mike had a sticky note covered with handwriting.

Initially, I worried this activity would take too much time and I'd fall behind the other world literature classes. However, the discussion allayed my fears. More students than usual participated. Many of them were confused in the same places, but I could tell by their questions and connections that they were beginning to construct meaning. Addressing their confusions, I delivered more information about canto 34 than if I had lectured.

A week later, the class began reading a play. In order to reinforce the concept of monitoring comprehension, I designed a highlighting activity that would help them be more aware of their thinking.

I passed out a pink and a yellow highlighter to each student, along with two pages photocopied from the play. For homework, I asked them to read the two pages and, as they read, to highlight every word, either in pink or yellow. If they understood what they read well enough to help someone in the class who didn't understand it, they should highlight that portion of the text in pink. If they read a portion that they didn't understand, they should highlight it in yellow.

The following morning students brought their highlighted pages back to class. I asked everyone to hold up their copy so they could see the various combinations of pink and yellow and realize that people have different areas of understanding. (I shared my highlighted photocopy of the pages as well.) I pointed out that everyone's paper looked different. Each of us had at least one part we understood as well as parts that caused confusion. I told them that together, we would construct meaning.

I read the pages aloud, occasionally stopping to ask who had highlighted a particular part in yellow. Several students would raise their hand. Since the students sitting at their desk with their hand down presumably understood the selection, I asked them to explain the passage to those who were confused.

I reminded the class that there was no penalty for highlighting in yellow: good readers know when they are confused. Likewise, there was no penalty for highlighting something in pink and misinterpreting it. The only way a student could fail was if they didn't highlight at all.

After reading the two pages, I asked the students to turn over their photocopies and write on the back whether this activity was helpful or had interfered with their understanding. Out of thirty-two students, twenty-eight believed it improved their comprehension. These were some of their comments:

> "The highlighting made me pay attention. I had to decide if I understood or if I was confused."

> "If I didn't understand something, I went back and reread. I thought about it and tried to make connections because I wanted to highlight my text in pink."

> "While I was doing this activity, my mind didn't wander, because I had to really think about what I was reading. The highlighting was helpful when we dis-

cussed it the following day, because I could return to the yellow areas and ask for help instead of wasting time searching for something I usually can't find."

"Highlighting helped me stay focused. Normally I just read quickly, and when I'm done I don't understand what I've read. Highlighting forces me to slow down and think about my reading."

If it is used too often, this activity can become monotonous. When used sparingly, it is a concrete way to help students take responsibility for monitoring their comprehension.

Are You Listening?

Many students enrolled in college preparatory classes are good readers and know when they are confused. In a sense, they listen to the thinking taking place in their heads. Struggling readers aren't always aware of their thinking. It's one reason they don't know they are confused.

"I don't hear any voices inside my head," Jeff admits one day. "There's nothing going on up there when I read. I just say the words."

Of course, Jeff has something going on "up there." He just isn't aware of it. The class laughs when I tell them I hear voices in my head all the time. They want to know what the "little voices" tell me to do. Undaunted by their insinuations that I'm mentally unbalanced, I continue.

"Actually, I have two types of voices in my head when I read. One voice, which I call my reciting voice, sounds like me reading. It just says words. The other voice is my conversation voice, and it helps me interact with what I am reading.

"When I am understanding my reading, I usually talk back to the author as if I'm having a conversation. For example, yesterday I was reading about a woman who left her three-year-old daughter behind when she escaped from Kosovo. The voice inside my head was sad and angry at the same time. I pictured my youngest daughter, Carrie, and wondered how this woman could leave her child. In my head, I wondered why she didn't do something to rescue the girl. I asked, 'What happened to the three-year-old after her mother left?' The article didn't tell me. Here it is the next day, and I'm still thinking about this little girl and her mother."

"You think about your reading even after you're done doing it?" asks Leigha.

"If I'm interacting with the text I do. I remember what I've read, and it sticks with me. If I just read the words, I usually forget what I've read right away."

"Maybe that's what happens to me," says Leigha. "I never remember what I read."

"What else does your conversation voice say?" asks Jeff.

"It tells me I am confused, and sometimes it asks a question or makes a connection. Other times, it makes a prediction or draws an inference. Lots of times my conversation voice argues with the book."

"What happens when you don't have a conversation voice?" asks Dan.

"You mean when I pronounce the words but have no idea what I've read?"

"Yeah, that's the one."

"I call that the reciting voice. It reminds me of the voice adults have in Charlie Brown cartoons: 'Wah Wah, Wah Wah Wahhh.' It sounds like me but doesn't carry meaning. I can hear myself reciting the words, but I'm not interacting with the text. I hear this voice when I read complicated directions or legal documents. I pronounce the words and hear the sound of my voice but I don't understand what I've read."

What Are We Supposed to Hear?

My classes are all too familiar with the meaningless reciting voice. Every one of them has experienced reading the words without interacting with the meaning. They need to know what the interacting conversation voice is like.

One day I decide to share an example of my thinking about the book we are currently reading, *Nightjohn,* by Gary Paulsen (1993). I divide the chalkboard into big boxes and turn to page 44. I read:

> But sometimes he [the plantation owner] likes to take the whip, and this time he whipped her until her back was ripped and bleeding. We had to watch.

I stop reading and begin to write on the chalkboard, jotting down the thinking that was taking place as I read the above passage. (It is important that I capture the thinking happening as I read, not the thinking generated as I write.) I write:

> I think the plantation owner made the slaves watch another slave being beaten so it would discourage them from breaking the rules. How cruel!

"This is what I was thinking as I read. Do you notice I made an inference? I was listening to the thinking taking place inside my head, and because of that I was able to respond to the book."

I continue reading about a slave named Alice who has been severely beaten because she has wandered up to the plantation house. I stop at the bottom of page 45. "This time my conversation voice is asking questions." I write the questions on the board:

Is Alice retarded or just defeated?

Why would she risk going where she wasn't supposed to?

I read on about the punishment dealt out to other slaves who dared to disobey. I stop at the bottom of page 48. I turn to the chalkboard and begin writing:

> I bet the master wants the slave left on the tree to serve as a warning to other runaways. No wonder some blacks hate whites. I think some African Americans blame whites today for what happened years ago. On the other hand, I'm not responsible for slavery. I didn't do anything. I am sickened when I read about the cruelties of slavery, and it makes me angry when people judge me because I am white. Some people assume I am a racist because I am white. That to me is prejudice.

Right away Leigha points out that my thinking strays from the book. "You're doing what I do."

"What's that?" I ask.

"Well, at first you are thinking about the book, and then you start thinking about something kind of related but not really."

"I see what you mean," I tell her. "At first, the voice inside my head is interacting with the story. Then I make a personal connection to the text, and I start to think about racism. The next thing I know, my thinking has started to drift away from the book."

Leigha readily admits she is guilty of the same behavior. "Lots of times I try to understand what I read, but I always end up thinking about something else."

"I know what you mean," says Jeff. "Sometimes thinking about my background knowledge causes me to think about things other than the book."

"That's okay, Jeff," I tell him. "As long as you know your mind is wandering, you can bring yourself back to the text. It's when you aren't aware that the voice in your head is off track that you're in trouble."

"Last night I read four pages before I realized I had no idea what I read," says Leigha.

"What happened?" I ask.

"Well," Leigha begins, "I was trying to read the chapter about the Boston Tea Party in my U.S. history book and I didn't have much background knowledge about it. I was trying to make connections between my life and the book. Since I didn't know anything about Boston or tea, I started thinking about parties. The next thing I knew, I was thinking about a party I went to last weekend. I thought about how much fun it was and realized I had already read four pages and had no idea what I'd read. I guess the voice inside my head was distracted."

Leigha has made an important distinction between interacting voices and distracting voices. An interacting voice encourages the reader to infer, make connections, ask questions, and synthesize information, while a distracting voice pulls the reader away from the text.

It isn't uncommon for a reader to be drawn away from the text. Oftentimes, a reader's background knowledge is triggered and his mind begins to wander. Leigha tried to relate the text to something she knew and was pulled off topic. It's understandable she was more interested in her social life than a dry history book. Leigha's background knowledge or lack of it drew her away from the reading. But if Leigha learns how to monitor the voices in her head, she will be able to pull herself back to the text and begin to develop a plan for getting unstuck. "The secret," as she herself says, "is knowing when the distracting voice goes too far."

The chart below can help you distinguish the differences between the different types of voices readers hear:

Reciting voice: The voice a reader hears when he is only reciting the words and not drawing meaning from the text.

Conversation voice: The voice that has a conversation with the text. It represents the reader's thinking as she talks back to the text in an interactive way. This voice can take two forms:

Interacting voice: The voice inside the reader's head that makes connections, asks questions, identifies confusions, agrees and disagrees with ideas. This voice deepens the reader's understanding of the text.

Distracting voice: The voice inside the reader's head that pulls him away from the meaning of the text. It begins a conversation with the reading but gets distracted by a connection, a question, or an idea. Soon the reader begins to think about something unrelated to the text.

It's About Listening

The next day, Dan walks into the classroom and says, "It seems to me that if I listen to the voices inside my head, I'll be able to tell if I am understanding what I am reading."

I smile. "You're right, Dan. When good readers listen to the different voices in their head, they know when they are stuck and they know how to get unstuck."

"Not this again," moans Dan.

"It's not that hard. Everyone has these voices. The trick is paying attention to them. Think of them as conversations between you and the book."

My students are skeptical. They want to believe thinking is taking place in their head, but they aren't sure how to identify it. I remind them of the sticky notes, reading logs, double-entry diaries, and coding sheets they've used. Each is a means of demonstrating the thinking that takes place as they read.

I also remind them of books we've read earlier in the year.

"Remember when we read *I Had Seen Castles,* by Cynthia Rylant, and how many of you compared it to John Hersey's *Hiroshima?* Several of you also compared the ideas in both these books to other wars you knew about. We discussed history, and how it repeats itself. Those conversations were possible because people were thinking as they read. They were listening to their inner voices and sharing their thoughts.

"And remember when I wanted the class to talk about Jack London's 'To Build a Fire'?"

"No one said anything after we read that story," Jim recalls.

"Why do you suppose that happened, Jim?"

"I didn't say anything because I was just reading the words," Jim answers.

"I didn't read for meaning either," says Kadee. "I only read it because I had to. I finished the last page and didn't remember a thing."

"That's a great example of listening only to your reciting voice," I say. "Kadee heard the words but didn't construct meaning. It's difficult to make connections, ask questions, infer, and help yourself get unstuck when you're only listening to your reciting voice."

"So, how do we do more than just read the words?" asks Leigha.

"Great question. When we learn about using background knowledge to make connections and how to ask questions so we can draw inferences, we are helping ourselves do more than just read the words. These are thinking strategies good readers consciously use to help themselves when their conversation voice shuts off. If a reader can recognize this, he can choose a thinking strategy to turn the conversation voice back on."

A comprehension constructor called Inner Voice (see Appendix B) is a good way to help students hold on to their thinking and practice listening to their inner voices:

> Stop at the end of each page designated in the boxes below and record what the voice in your head is saying. Identify whether the voice is just reciting the words, being distracted, or interacting with the text.

Throughout the year, I refer to the voices inside my students' heads when they read and encourage them to use the voices to construct meaning. By the end of the year, students easily recognize the voices and are able to describe what the voices do.

Nikki tells the class she relies on her inner voices in chemistry. "That's a hard class," she says. "Listening to my inner voice helps me know when I am confused. When I don't remember something I've read, I know I was listening to the reciting voice and I have to go back and reread. My conversation voice tells me to ask questions or make predictions. When I pay attention to the voices in my head, I am more involved in the reading."

James tells us that whenever he starts to drift off, his inner voice says, "Wait a minute. I don't get this. I better go back and fix my meaning."

Melissa relies on her inner voices in algebra 2. She tells the class it helps her understand story problems, that she is able to make connections and estimate what an appropriate answer would be.

These students expect to gain meaning from their reading. They know that if they listen to the voices inside their head, they will be able to make decisions about their reading. They understand that it is their job to know when meaning is interrupted and that only they can monitor their comprehension because the last thing they want is for any teacher to read their mind!

What Works

1. Share real-life examples of professions that require practitioners to be aware of their thinking. Point out athletes, musicians, and people they know who, in order to be successful at what they do, must monitor their thinking. Help students see that readers aren't the only ones who have to think while doing "their thing." Show examples of text that you understand as well as text that is confusing. Point out that a reader can't help himself if he hasn't recognized that meaning has been interrupted. Let students know that it isn't your job alone to monitor their understanding. Relinquish the majority of responsibility to them.

TEACHING POINT: Good readers know it is their job to monitor their comprehension. They know when they are making sense of their reading, and they know when they are confused. Good readers don't disguise or ignore their confusion. They acknowledge it so they can eliminate it.

2. Help students recognize the six signals (see page 38) that indicate confusion. Point out how you know when you are confused, and post the six indicators in your classroom.

TEACHING POINT: Good readers know that when the following behaviors occur, it is time to stop and make a plan to repair meaning:

- The inner voice inside the reader's head stops its conversation with the text, and the reader only hears his voice pronouncing the words.
- The camera inside the reader's head shuts off, and the reader can no longer visualize what is happening as she reads.
- The reader's mind begins to wander, and he catches himself thinking about something far removed from the text.
- The reader cannot remember or retell what she has read.
- The reader is not getting his clarifying questions answered.
- Characters are reappearing in the text and the reader doesn't recall who they are.

3. Give students opportunities to isolate their confusion so they can begin repairing the breakdown in meaning. Teach them how to put a sticky note next to a passage that causes confusion so they can return to it later and try to clarify it. For homework, photocopy a portion of a reading assignment and let students use pink and yellow highlighters to mark places they understand (pink) and places that are confusing (yellow).

TEACHING POINT: Good readers know how to identify their confusion so they can help themselves get unstuck. If they are unable to help themselves, they know they can ask an expert.

4. Explain to students that readers hear voices when they read. Share the voices you hear when you read. Point out how sometimes the voice in your head only recites the words. (It's important to acknowledge that this happens even to you.) Tell students how you turn this reciting voice into a conversation voice. Explain that sometimes the conversation voice distracts you from the meaning, and show students how you bring yourself back to the text.

TEACHING POINT: Good readers listen to the voices in their head to help them know when they are understanding and when they are confused. Good readers know that sometimes the voice helps the reader interact with the text and sometimes the voice pulls the reader away from the text. Good readers know how to bring themselves back to their reading by selecting a thinking strategy that will repair meaning.

5

Fix It!

When I get stuck, I quit reading.

Luke, grade 9

Frankness like Luke's surprises me. Is he lazy, or does he quit reading because he doesn't know how to help himself? "Luke," I ask, "why don't you try to get unstuck?"

Without hesitating, he answers, "Because nothing I try helps me. Rereading is a waste of time."

"Try another fix-up strategy then."

"What's a fix-up strategy?" he wants to know.

"A fix-up strategy," I tell him, "is something you use to help yourself get unstuck when you are reading confusing text."

This time, Luke pauses before he answers. "When I was younger, I used to try sounding words out but that didn't really help."

"Did you learn to do anything else?"

"No, not really."

"Hmm." I survey the faces in the room and ask, "Does anyone else have a strategy he or she could suggest to Luke?"

"I don't do anything," brags Kayla.

"You don't do anything?" I ask.

"Nope, I keep reading and hope it makes sense when I am done."

"And what if it doesn't?"

"Then, oh well."

A sense of panic washes over me, as I realize these kids don't care whether their reading makes sense or not. When it doesn't, they simply quit. I realized long ago that most struggling readers weren't going to love reading enough to choose it as a leisurely pastime. However, electing to quit when text becomes difficult is a choice that could have serious consequences. In a few short years, these students will be on their own. They will have to read apartment leases, car-loan contracts, income tax forms, and material associated with their jobs. It's one thing to quit reading a chapter out of a textbook and fail a test. It's quite a different matter to quit reading an income tax form and miss out on a refund. Automatically abandoning a text because it doesn't make sense is going to make life for a struggling reader even more difficult.

Rereading Is Only the Beginning

Upon further investigation, I learn that many students have tried to help themselves repair confusion. Unfortunately, their plans aren't very strategic. Jenny, a freshman with perfect nails, is required by her father to read ten pages of something every night. She claims that when she reads, she becomes sleepy. In order to get through the ten pages, Jenny polishes one fingernail per page. She is motivated to stay awake because if she doesn't, the polish will nick and she will have to start over.

Mark claims he rereads everything one hundred times. Amber tells the class that when she gets stuck she looks over the assignment and "tries to figure it out." Brandon says he thinks about his background knowledge, then rereads. If that doesn't work, he quits. I'm not sure Brandon truly understands how to use fix-up strategies. I suspect he's parroting comments I've made in class.

Everyone in my classes seems to know how to reread. However, several admit they seldom do it, because they are slow readers and it would take too long. Others say they are lucky to get through an assignment once, let alone read something again. Some students suggest asking for help. When I ask from whom they could get help, they say, "The teacher." But most adolescents are expected to do their school reading at home. Since teachers aren't around when students do the majority of their reading, asking the teacher for help is an ineffective plan.

Other kids reveal that when they get stuck, they think harder. I know that strategy. It was taught to me by my fifth-grade teacher, who should have retired five years earlier. We were doing fractions and I was struggling to learn how to find common denominators.

After many incorrect attempts, I decided to ask for help. My teacher kneeled down beside my desk and through clenched teeth said, "Think harder!" As she watched me work, I did think harder. I thought how bad her coffee breath smelled, how much I hated math, and how I would wait until I got home to ask for help. Thinking harder about something I didn't understand in the first place wasn't really a strategy I could sink my teeth into. Neither can my students.

Strategies to "Fix Up" Confusion

The next morning, Amber saunters into the room and asks a question that is music to my ears: "What are we supposed to do when we get stuck reading?"

"Funny you should ask," I say. "I've got a whole list of strategies readers can try when they get stuck."

By now, the majority of the class is eavesdropping on our conversation. Many of them seem excited to learn there are other ways than rereading to get unstuck. I pass out a sheet listing the following fix-up strategies:

- Make a connection between the text and:

  Your life.

  Your knowledge of the world.

  Another text.
- Make a prediction.
- Stop and think about what you have already read.
- Ask yourself a question and try to answer it.
- Reflect in writing on what you have read.
- Visualize.
- Use print conventions.
- Retell what you've read.
- Reread.
- Notice patterns in text structure.
- Adjust your reading rate: slow down or speed up.

My students look at the list.

"Good readers actually do these things?" Jeff asks.

"When they get confused they have to do something to get rid of the misunderstanding," I say. "They can't ignore it, or the problem will get worse. Do you think good readers understand everything they read the first time?"

Jeff gives me a funny look—this is exactly what he does think. He assumes proficient readers automatically comprehend everything they read. He can't believe they also struggle to understand difficult text.

Then Leigha whines, "I don't even know what these things mean!" I pause, and explain that we will begin the work of understanding what these strategies mean. It's work that will require teacher modeling and practice that will take many weeks.

Make a Connection Between the Text and Your Life, Your Knowledge of the World, or Another Text

Sometimes a reader has information about a topic in his head that isn't being used. When brought to bear, this background knowledge can be a powerful tool, helping the reader repair meaning. Good readers know that using knowledge to make a connection will help them understand their reading better. They use memories, personal experiences, information about the subject, the author's style, and textual organization to help them visualize, predict, ask questions, infer, stay focused, and remember what they have read.

Text connections can give a reader insights into a character's motive. Sometimes recalling factual information helps the reader understand why an event is taking place. Remembering another story with a similar plot enables the reader to anticipate action. Identifying an author's writing style or the organizational pattern of a text helps the reader understand what the author is saying.

Make a Prediction

Good readers anticipate what's coming next. Based on what they've already read, readers expect certain new events to occur. When an event doesn't match a prediction, readers rethink and revise their thinking. More important, they are alerted to possible confusion. Sometimes misreading words throws the prediction off. When readers predict, they are aware meaning is breaking down. Instead of ignoring an incorrect prediction, they get back into the action by making a new guess. Predicting jolts readers back on track. It keeps them involved so they aren't surprised by incorrect conclusions.

Stop and Think About What You Have Already Read

This one is so easy most students ignore it. Yet it is one of the most useful fix-up strategies of all. Good readers ponder what they have read. They connect newly acquired knowledge with information they already have. Stopping and thinking gives readers time to synthesize new information. It allows opportunities to ask questions, visualize, and determine what is important in the text.

Ask a Question

Good readers ask themselves questions when they read. Curious about the answers, they continue reading. Sometimes these questions are answered directly in the text, and meaning is clarified. Typically, clarifying questions are about a character, setting, event, or process: *who, what, when,* and *where* questions.

Other times, answers to readers' questions aren't found in the text. These are pondering questions that don't always have simple answers.

They ask *how* and *why*. In these cases, the reader is forced to go beyond the words to find the answer, either by drawing an inference or by going to another source.

Struggling readers sometimes expect to find all the answers to their questions in the text. These readers often miss test questions like "What's the best title for this piece?" or "What's the main idea?" They don't realize that the answers can be found by using clues from the text and their background knowledge to draw an inference. Many secondary students think this is cheating or wasting time.

Readers who ask questions and know where the answers to their questions are to be found are more likely to have a richer read, to infer, to draw conclusions, and regain control of their reading.

Write About What You've Read

Writing down what they think about what they've read allows readers to clarify their thinking. It is an opportunity to reflect. Readers better understand their reading when they have written about it. The writing may be a summary or a response. Sometimes just jotting down a few notes will clarify meaning.

Visualize

When meaning breaks down, good readers consciously create images in their head to help them make sense of what the words are saying. They use movies, television, and life to help them picture what is happening. When a reader can visualize what is happening, comprehension improves. Secondary students are bombarded with visual images. These images can help readers make a video in their head. If they can "see it," they often understand it.

Last summer, I worked with a young man named Jason, who was soon to be a senior. His mother was concerned that he wouldn't do well in English because he didn't remember what he read. For an hour a week I helped him learn how to use background knowledge and create visual images while he read.

As a homework assignment, I asked him to read a controversial magazine article about Area 51 (a suspected top-secret government research and development site investigating UFOs), thinking he would have no trouble relating it to one of the movies he had seen about UFOs. He came back the next week complaining that he didn't understand what he read because he didn't have any background knowledge about the topic.

I asked if he had seen any television shows or movies that might help him visualize what was happening. Jason looked up from the magazine and said, "Yeah, I saw a movie with Will Smith about aliens that were attacking the earth." Then he said something that really surprised me. "I didn't think I should really use movies when I'm reading. Isn't that cheating?"

"Cheating?" I asked incredulously. "What do you mean?"

Jason explained that his teachers often complained that students watched too much TV and wasted their time at movie theaters. Even though the movie he was remembering featured Area 51, he didn't think he should use it to do "schoolwork."

Jason remembered the movie in great detail. He described the desert and the top security surrounding the area. When we went back to reread the article, I asked Jason to use those images to help him visualize the words in the text. Almost automatically, he begin to comprehend parts that were confusing before. He now understood why there was no water in "Groom Lake," that it was so named because it once was a lake during prehistoric times. He could now visualize a top security facility in the middle of nowhere and was even able to infer that it was where it was because of its inaccessibility. Once Jason realized it was all right to use his vast repertoire of video images, he was able to better visualize the words he was reading.

Use Print Conventions

Key words, bold print, italicized words, capital letters, and punctuation are all used to enhance understanding. Conventions of print help the author convey intent. They help the reader determine what is important and what the author values. Conventions of print give the reader insight into voice inflections and how the author wants the piece to sound. Poor readers often ignore conventions because they are unaware of their function. Pointing out conventions will not only improve reading comprehension but also help students use these same conventions to convey meaning when they write.

Retell What You've Read

Taking a moment to retell what has been read helps the reader reflect. It activates background knowledge and also provides a check on whether the reader is understanding. When readers can't retell what they read, it is an indication that their minds have been wandering or confusion has set in. Asking *What have I just read?* refreshes the reader's memory and prepares her to read the next part. This is a useful strategy when returning to reading after some time has passed. Students frequently read something and then don't pick up the material again for several days. Teaching students to quickly recall what they have already read before starting new material can save time. Readers who don't recall what they have read before beginning new text end up doing it while they are reading the new material and therefore don't pay attention to it.

Reread

When meaning breaks down, readers can stop and decide whether there is something in the text they can reread that will help them understand the piece better. Since this is the one strategy most readers know automatically, it needs little explaining. An important aspect to remember is that a student doesn't have to reread everything for the strategy to be helpful. Sometimes rereading portions of the text—a sentence, or even just a word—can enhance comprehension. Struggling readers tend to think rereading means they have to reread everything.

Notice Patterns in Text Structure

Genres have specific organizational patterns. Recognizing how a piece is organized helps readers locate information more quickly. When my daughters played high school volleyball, I relied on the organizational pattern of the local newspaper to find out quickly whether they were mentioned in an article. I knew the sports section was toward the back of the paper and that every Thursday the paper featured high school athletics after professional and collegiate sports. I didn't have to read the entire newspaper—or the entire sports section—to find out the information I wanted.

Some struggling readers believe that they have to read everything from cover to cover, even nonfiction. Taking time to explain how a piece is organized helps students figure out where information is found. It helps them determine what is important. When meaning breaks down, readers can stop and think how the text is organized and see whether there is something in the organizational pattern that will help them understand the piece.

Adjust Reading Rate: Slow Down or Speed Up

Contrary to what struggling readers think, good readers don't read everything fast. They adjust their rate to meet the demands of the task. Many secondary students read course textbooks at the same rate they read their favorite magazine. Good readers slow down when something is difficult or unfamiliar. They realize that in order to construct meaning, their rate must decrease. They also know that it's okay to read faster when something is familiar or boring. Reading faster sometimes forces the brain to stay engaged. Good readers select a rate based on the difficulty of the material, their purpose in reading it, and their familiarity with the topic.

Not all fix-up strategies will work all the time. Some work better than others depending on the nature of your confusion. It is important that students know that when good readers get stuck, they don't quit. They stop and decide how to repair their confusion. The more plans readers have for reconstructing comprehension, the more likely they are to stick with their reading.

Driving and Reading

My friend and colleague Laura Benson once used a metaphor comparing reading with driving a car. It hit home, and I've embellished it to help students understand how important monitoring comprehension is and how useful fix-up strategies can be.

When I drive, I have a destination in mind. I am very conscious of what is going on around me. I monitor my speed. I compare it with the posted limits. I know to slow down for speed traps, and I know when I can exceed the speed limit without risking danger to myself or others. When a song comes on the radio that I like, I turn it up. When a song comes on that I don't like, I change the station. I watch the gas and oil gauges to make sure they are in acceptable ranges. I look in the mirrors so I know where other cars are around me. As long as I am heading toward my destination, I keep driving.

However, if I encounter difficulty, I stop and try to correct the problem. If I get a flat tire or I am caught speeding I *can't* keep driving unless I want to make my situation worse. Driving on a flat can bend the rim and foul up the alignment. Ignoring the flashing red lights of a patrol car can land me in jail. There are no two ways around it. I can't keep going. I need to stop and plan what to do next.

This plan doesn't need to be elaborate, but it does have to meet the demands of the situation. My thinking needs to be flexible; I might have to try a few different strategies before I find one that works. I have to do more than sit in the car and cry. Crying won't help me get back on the road. I need to weigh my options and decide which one will help me the most.

If I want to fix the flat tire, the obvious choice would be to change it. Unfortunately, this won't work for me because I don't even know where the spare is, let alone the circular wrench that gets the tire off the car. Changing the tire isn't a plan that will help me. But I can't just sit there. I need to try something else.

I could use the cell phone to call someone, but when I reach into the glove compartment to retrieve it, I realize this plan won't work either. Someone has used the phone and has neglected to return it. I can decide to walk to a gas station, but I notice that it is getting dark and I am in a part of town that isn't safe; walking wouldn't be smart. Finally, I decide to raise the hood of the car, lock the doors, turn on my flashers, and wait for a police officer to come to my aid. The point is, I don't give up. When one plan doesn't work, I try something else.

Monitoring comprehension and using fix-up strategies is a lot like driving. Good readers expect to arrive at meaning, just as good drivers expect to arrive at their destination. A reader's ultimate purpose is to gain meaning. In order to do this, readers must monitor their comprehension, and when meaning breaks down, they need to repair it.

Repairing Confusion

Students need opportunities to select fix-up strategies based on the nature of the problem. Not every fix-up strategy works in every instance. Before students can use fix-up strategies flexibly and automatically, they need to recognize confusion and analyze what is causing the confusion. Only then can readers choose how they will try to repair meaning.

Readers who encounter an unknown word know that rereading the word over and over again isn't going to help. They may ask someone the meaning or look the word up in the dictionary. Circumstances dictate which fix-up strategy to use. If the reader is alone, she can't ask for help. If she doesn't have a dictionary or is too lazy to look up the word, she has to find another way to help herself. Perhaps she reads around the unknown word and tries to make a logical guess about its meaning. She may decide that the word is unimportant and consciously skip it. She may conclude that unless the word reappears, it isn't necessary to the understanding of the piece. If the word does reappear, she may decide it is important. She can flag it so she can talk to her teacher about it the next day. A reader who is aware of all of these options can attack her comprehension problem.

Another day, another class. I refer to the list of fix-up strategies on the board and begin working through several students' comprehension problems.

"Jim's problem is he doesn't know what *pariah* means. What could he do?"

"Just skip it," says Brandon.

"He could just skip it," I say, "but what if it is a word he really needs to know?"

"I could look it up," says Jim. Unfortunately, at the time our room was equipped with third-grade dictionaries that had few polysyllabic words and Jim was unable to find his unknown word.

"Okay, now what do you do?" I ask.

Jim looks at the list of fix-up strategies. "I could ask someone for help, or I could just skip it."

Sensing that Jim is feeling he is working too hard to find the meaning of the word, I tell him, "A pariah is a social outcast." Jim smiles and writes the definition on a sticky note. I don't want to stop here, though. I tell the class that sometimes it is okay to decide to skip the word. However, if the word keeps appearing, it's probably important. Asking someone what a word means is okay too, but if no one is around to ask, it is important to know other ways to figure out unknown words. Here are a few strategies to try:

1. Look at the structure of the word. Is there a familiar prefix, root, or suffix? Teachers don't teach structural analysis because it is fun and exhilarating. They teach it because sometimes readers can use this information to crack difficult words and approximate meanings.

2. Use the glossary if there is one. Let's be honest. Most people don't look up every unknown word they come to. However, glossaries are handy and much easier to use than an unwieldy dictionary.

3. Read the words around the unknown word. Can another word be substituted? Take a guess. What word would make sense there?

4. Write the word down on a sticky note. The next day in class, ask the teacher.

Next, Amber reads a paragraph aloud to the class. "When I read this, I was thinking about something else," she says.

"Amber caught herself thinking about something other than the book. I do that too," I confess. "Amber recognizes her mind is wandering and instead of reading on she stops to fix her problem." I ask Amber how she knows she is stuck.

"I was reading about the slaves. The text made me think they were treated like animals. Animals started me thinking about my dog at home, who is about to have puppies. When I realized what I was thinking about, I had read the whole page and didn't remember a thing."

Again, I refer to the list of fix-up strategies on the board. "What can Amber try to get unstuck?"

Kandice says, "Reread."

Even though Amber says, "Good idea," I can tell she's not satisfied with the answer. I ask the class, "What else can she try?"

Curtis suggests that Amber go back to the last part she remembers. As she rereads she should consciously try to make a picture in her head. "Try to visualize what's happening in the book," says Curtis. "It might make it easier to pay attention if you have a picture in your head."

Amber is ready to reread. She has a concrete plan of attack.

Finally DeAndre, who is reading *Nightjohn* (Paulsen 1993), says he is confused by the characters' dialogue. He doesn't know who is talking. His confusion has a lot to do with his inattentiveness to the conventions of print. He is not using punctuation to aid meaning. I point out that quotation marks and new paragraphs are used to help the reader know who is talking without putting *he said, she said* in all the time. When a new character talks, a new paragraph begins. Quotation marks separate one person's speeches from another's.

I ask DeAndre to go back to where the book last made sense. I ask him to begin rereading this part out loud. After a sentence or two I stop him and ask, "Who is talking now?" He tells me it is Sarney, a young slave girl. DeAndre continues, but I can tell by the way he is reading that he has no idea who is speaking. I ask him who is talking now.

"I don't know. It is either Nightjohn or Sarney," he answers.

I point out the quotation marks and ask DeAndre to return to the point where Sarney last spoke. I ask him to slow down and look for paragraph changes. DeAndre adjusts his speed and forces himself to notice paragraph changes and quotation marks. He begins rereading, after saying to himself, "Okay, Sarney is talking now." He moves on and says, "This is Nightjohn talking." Noticing quotation marks and other print conventions make it easy to tell who is talking.

Practice Makes Perfect

After students know how to recognize their confusion and which fix-up strategies are available for them to use, they can practice their thinking using the following Comprehension Constructor:

I am confused by (copy directly from the text whatever your confusion is): _____ Page _____

I am confused because (try to diagnose why you are confused):

_____

I will try (record different fix-up strategies you try):

_____

I understand (explain how your understanding is deeper as a result of the fix-up strategies you've used):

_____

_____

Before giving this Comprehension Constructor to students to complete on their own, I explain how to complete each line using something I am reading. On the first line, for example, students are tempted to write, "I'm confused because it's hard." I model on a transparency of the Comprehension Constructor how to copy the confusion directly from the text. Later, Joey, a ninth grader reading *Nightjohn,* writes on the first line, "My job was to spit chewing tobacco on the roses."

On the second line students are tempted to write, "I am confused because I don't get it." I explain that this line is a place for students to analyze why they think they are confused. Joey writes, "I am confused because I've never heard of spitting chewing tobacco on plants to kill bugs."

The third line is reserved for fix-up strategies students try to clear up their confusion. Joey writes, "I will try to get unstuck by rereading, making connections, stopping and thinking."

The last line is an opportunity for students to synthesize their thinking and decide how using fix-up strategies repaired their confusion. Joey writes, "I understand that chewing tobacco is made from tobacco leaves and water. Saliva is generated and the tobacco juice will kill the bugs on the roses because it will eat their stomachs away. That's why you spit the tobacco out instead of swallowing it. If the tobacco hurts people's stomachs, it must be bad for bugs."

Even though Joey wasn't exactly correct in his theory of tobacco and pest control, he was able to repair his confusion enough to keep going. Joey is a reader who typically quits when confusion sets in. With this Comprehension Constructor he was able to pull himself through a few thinking processes in order to fix up meaning. He did it all by himself. I didn't intervene and tell him how to get unstuck. By focusing on the process, Joey was able to repair his own confusion.

■ ■ ■ ■ ■ ■ *What Works*

1. Share material you find confusing. Remind students that even good readers get confused when they read. Demonstrate what you do when

you recognize a problem in your comprehension. Show students how to flag interruptions in meaning. Try reading aloud a difficult piece of text and have students record the fix-up strategies you use to regain meaning.

TEACHING POINT: Good readers isolate confusion and make a plan to repair meaning. They know that if they continue reading without doing anything to help themselves, their confusion will get worse.

2. Give a list of fix-up strategies to your students. Ask them to use these strategies while reading their class assignments. Ask them to try at least one fix-up strategy before you help them clear up their confusion.

TEACHING POINT: Good readers don't quit when they become confused. They use fix-up strategies to repair confusion.

3. Demonstrate how listening to the voices in your head helps you know which fix-up strategy to use. Let students know that not every fix-up strategy works in every situation. Tell them that it is okay to abandon a fix-up strategy if it isn't helping.

TEACHING POINT: Good readers use fix-up strategies flexibly. When one doesn't work, they try another one.

6

Connecting the New to the Known

When I read Bean Trees, *I made connections between my life and Taylor's. I wondered what I would do and how my family would act in the same situation. I connect everything I read to my life. Thinking about my life helps me understand what I read.*

Becky, grade 12

Last fall, I observed a chemistry class of juniors and seniors. They were balancing chemical equations at their desk and taking turns solving them at the front of the room. One young man in particular was having difficulty matching his answers to the correct ones on the board. His teacher surveyed his paper and quietly reminded him to use what he knew about simple algebra. I was surprised by his reaction. "Algebra?" he asked. "This is chemistry! What do I need algebra for?" I continued watching him as he muttered to himself, perplexed at the idea of using math in a science class.

The bell rang, and I never saw the student again. I thought how powerful it would have been for the teacher to stop what she was doing and model the connection between algebra and chemistry for the entire class. Perhaps she assumed everyone understood the relationship between math and science. I wondered whether the chemistry student used the information his teacher had given him to finish the assignment. More than likely he forgot about it the minute he left the room. Watching both student and teacher neglect such an obvious link made me think many students could benefit from instruction that explicitly pointed out patterns and connections.

For years, I assumed students connected information they learned in one class to information they learned in another. I expected my students to use what they learned from me to help them not only in other classes but also in the real world. But my experience working with adolescent readers showed me this wasn't always the case. Many students ignored what they knew and dove right into new material without considering their background knowledge. They didn't know that the information in their head is a powerful resource when reading difficult text.

Blurring Boundaries

Middle and secondary schools, by their very nature, isolate information. The short periods of instruction often compartmentalize thinking; as students rush from class to class every fifty minutes, they box up their knowledge according to the course. Some students may begin their day with algebra and then race to English. After English they head to earth science and then on to U.S. history. It's as if students are expected to switch their brains from one subject to the next in the ten minutes between periods. It's no wonder many students have difficulty connecting information from one content area to another.

Rarely do teachers take time to blur the boundaries between content areas. If students can be shown how knowledge interrelates, they can use the information taught in one class to help them with the material in another. The burden of covering vast amounts of content will be eased if teachers work together, showing students how to use the information they already know. Good readers rely on background knowledge to help them make sense of text. Chemistry students who use what they know about algebra are more likely to be successful at balancing equations than students who ignore math. Someone who argues *I'm in science therefore I don't need math* isn't very strategic. So too, ignoring existing prior knowledge puts readers at a great disadvantage. They limit their success because they aren't using everything they have available to them. They seem to attack unfamiliar content without considering prior knowledge, the author, the genre, or the historical background. It is vital that students make connections when they read. It's up to teachers to show them how.

Reading teachers have known for years that information is best remembered when it is connected to a reader's background knowledge and prior experience. I define *background knowledge* for my students as the information a reader has in her head. It is more than memory. It is a storehouse of knowledge that provides the reader with an assortment of information. Background knowledge is a repository of memories, experiences, and facts. When information is read in isolation and not connected to existing knowledge, it is forgotten and deemed unimportant. Calling on existing knowledge and experiences is crucial if readers are to assimilate new information.

After reading the short vignette "My Name" from *The House on Mango Street* by Sandra Cisneros (1991), Estrella, a struggling ninth grader, writes, "The girl in the story wants to change her name. I'd like to change my name too, because people say it is funny. I understand how the little girl in the story feels." As an aside, she turns to the friend sitting next to her. "It's weird. I only remember the stuff I connect to." Estrella's connection to the story not only helps her remember what she reads but also helps her empathize with the character. Once students begin using their background knowledge, they are more likely to draw inferences, ask questions, and make comparisons and contrasts.

This Is Language Arts—Who Cares About Social Studies?

Good readers know how to "wake up" and use the information they have about a topic in order to help them understand what they are reading. However, many readers need to be shown how to do this. My daughter Sara was one such reader when she was in middle school. It never crossed her mind to use information in one class to help her in another.

One afternoon, Sara stormed into the house, threw a book on the table, and on her way to the phone announced, "I have to read forty pages of this stupid book by tomorrow."

I continued cleaning the kitchen counter and asked her what the book was about. She rolled her eyes and said, "I don't know. Some war. The Revolutionary War? The Civil War? Who cares?"

I knew that if Sara was going to understand this book she had to figure out what war the book was about. I picked it up, glanced at the cover, and saw that it was *April Morning* (Fast 1961), a classic Revolutionary War story. "How can I help?" I asked.

"How should I know?" she shrugged. "You're the reading specialist."

"Okay." I took a big breath. "Let's think about what you're studying in school. Is there anything you're learning in your other classes that may help you understand this book? What about social studies?"

"This book is for language arts, Mom. It doesn't matter what we are doing in social studies."

"Maybe not," I said, "but just in case, tell me what you know."

Stubbornly, Sara said, "We're learning about the Revolutionary War." Period.

"So, what do you know about the Revolutionary War?" I asked.

"Not very much," she whined. "I know about the colonists and King George. Oh yeah, the Lobster Backs. That's what the colonists called King George's soldiers." Sara then explained the Boston Tea Party and why the colonists were fighting for independence. Actually, she knew quite a bit about the Revolutionary War, and once she began talking about it she surprised herself with just how much she knew and how this knowledge would help her read the novel.

Teachers have an important role helping students acquire new knowledge. However, their job is easier if they first teach students how to use information they already know. Sara had enough background knowledge to understand the book. She just wasn't using it.

I knew that if I read the forty pages with Sara I would help her this one time, but it wasn't going to make her a better reader. I wanted to teach her a strategy that she could apply to other situations. In other words, I wanted to teach Sara, not *April Morning.* Since good readers make connections between the new and the known, I decided I could make a significant improvement in Sara's ability to comprehend if I pointed this out. I explained that I was reasonably sure her teachers had purposely planned to have students learn about the Revolutionary War by studying it in social studies while reading a historical fiction novel in language arts. Her teachers were giving students more than one opportunity to learn content.

I asked Sara to think about her social studies class. I reminded her that she knew a lot about the Revolutionary War and that if she used this information as she read *April Morning,* her comprehension would improve. She smiled. It was something she could easily do. Together, we start reading the novel aloud. Almost immediately, Sara began making connections and soon was able to understand what was just moments before a difficult text.

Of course, Sara needed more practice before she was able to make connections between new and known information on her own. She needed more teacher modeling and more time practicing the strategy of connecting the new to the known before she could do it as a matter of course in all her classes.

Fortunately, Sara's teachers understood the value of teaching interdisciplinary units. Her social studies teacher built background knowledge while her language arts teacher reinforced it. Unfortunately, neither teacher explained how the two content areas supported each other. I suspect Sara wasn't the only one in her seventh-grade class missing the connection.

Two simple ways to help students make connections between the new and the known are:

1. Create a Venn diagram showing students how subject areas overlap and how they are different. A Venn diagram can also be used to bridge information between textbook chapters or linked novels.

2. Jot a topic of study on the chalkboard (for example, *the Revolutionary War*). While taking attendance or dealing with some other preparatory task, have students come up and jot down what they know about the topic. Kids love this. It's a great way to call up students' background knowledge as well as inform students who don't know much about the current topic.

Don't assume students are connecting information just because the connection seems obvious. Explicitly point out patterns and similarities. The few minutes it takes to show students relationships among content, text structure, and factual information is well worth the time.

Another assumption I am guilty of making is thinking students know more than they do. This is particularly true when I've taught the same novel several years in a row or used the same textbook year after year.

It's easy to forget what it was like to read something for the first time. Textbooks are often cursory, and students typically don't have the background to fill in the blanks the same way teachers do. It's easy to think students are leaping along with you when in actuality they are clinging for dear life to the side of a cliff.

Readers benefit significantly from instruction that elucidates cognitive processes. Take time to notice how you as an expert reader of the material make use of existing knowledge. Do you jog your memory before you read? Do you make connections as you read? Do you use these connections to help yourself visualize or infer? Ask yourself how your reading changes when you have a lot of information about the topic versus little or none. By noticing your processes as a reader who connects existing knowledge to new knowledge, you will be well on the way to teaching your students how to use the same strategy.

Personal Knowledge or Personal Experience?

Teaching students how to use existing background knowledge is relatively easy. The difficulty arises when students claim to have little or no background knowledge and refuse to make connections. Students who do this usually confuse *personal knowledge* with *personal experience*. Randi Allison, a wonderful literacy teacher I know in Colorado, clarified the difference between the two for me. She explained that personal knowledge is information readers have from stories, movies, television, books, anything that helps them acquire information secondhand. Personal experience is information readers have gained from direct experience. Naturally, students will be asked to read lots of pieces of text to which they can bring no related personal experience. Usually, however, they have personal knowledge from movies, television, or other texts they've read.

For example, I haven't personally experienced war, but I have a lot of personal knowledge about war. I have seen movies about war, watched documentaries, talked with veterans, and read books. True, my concept of war is not as visceral as that of someone who has lived it. Nevertheless, there is a lot of information I can bring to a piece about war that will help me understand it more deeply.

Unfortunately, when students read about an unfamiliar topic they often become lost because they assume they don't know anything about the topic. This is especially true if they are reading about something that occurred before they were born. Many secondary readers complain that they don't know anything about the topics they read in science and social studies. They have difficulty relating to the information and they can see no relevance to their lives. They become bored and quickly abandon the text. Even when the subject is interesting, it seldom holds their attention, because they aren't making connections.

One of the best ways to help readers interact with the text is to show them that they have something in common with it. Marking text is an access tool that forces readers to make connections when they read. Make a transparency of a page from whatever material is being read—a textbook, a novel, a poem. Then read portions of the text out loud and share the connections you make with the class.

When I read familiar material, my connections are personal and very sophisticated. When I encounter difficult material or material containing new information, my connections are much simpler and less sophisticated. Nevertheless, I model how I am able to connect to the piece in some fashion. As I read aloud, I stop whenever I encounter something that reminds me of something in my life—a memory or recollection of an experience. Perhaps the connection is with a fact I remember. Maybe I am reminded of a song or another story. I stop reading and talk out loud about what my connection is. I mark the part in the text that causes me to make a connection and jot down what the lines remind me of. Below is an example of how I've marked a poem by Naomi Shihab Nye called "Valentine for Ernest Mann":

Valentine for Ernest Mann

You can't order a poem like you order a taco
Walk up to the counter, say, "I'll take two"
and expect it to be handed back to you
on a shiny plate.

> BK This reminds me of a drive-thru in San Diego. It's right by the beach and swimmers can walk up to the window.

Still I like your spirit.
Anyone who says, "Here's my address,
write me a poem," deserves something in reply.
So I'll tell you a secret instead:
poems hide. In the bottoms of our shoes,
drifting across our ceilings the moment
before we wake up. What we have to do
is live in a way that lets us find them.

Once I knew a man who gave his wife
two skunks for a valentine.
He couldn't understand why she was crying.

> BK This reminds me of the Christmas I received a cappuccino maker.

"I thought they had such beautiful eyes."
And he was serious. He was a serious man
who lived in a serious way. Nothing was ugly
just because the world said so. He really
liked those skunks. So, he re-invented them
as valentines and they became beautiful.
At least, to him. And the poems that had been hiding
in the eyes of skunks for centuries
crawled out and curled up at his feet.

Maybe if we re-invent whatever our lives give us
we find poems. Check your garage, the odd sock
in your drawer, the person you almost like, but not quite.
And let me know.

BK This reminds me of when I thought black oil was beautiful.

My connections are personal and relevant only to me, but they help me as a reader in several ways: (1) I am able to create visual pictures in my head; (2) I am more interested in reading the poem because I interact with the poet instead of just "barking" at the print; and (3) I bring meaning to the words instead of expecting meaning to reside in the words.

After a bit of modeling, students are ready to try making connections on their own. When readers who claim to have no background knowledge consciously try to make connections, they usually find they do indeed have something in common with the text.

Colleen Buddy categorizes three types of connections readers make: text to self, text to world, and text to text (see Figure 6.1). (See also Keene and Zimmermann 1997 and Harvey and Goudvis 2000.)

Figure 6.1

Text-to-Reader Connections

1. Text to self: Connections between the text and the reader's experiences and memories. The more experiences and memories a reader has about a topic, the easier the material is to read.

2. Text to world: Connections the reader makes between the text and what he knows about the world (facts and information).

3. Text to text: Connections the reader makes between two or more types of texts. The reader may make connections relative to plot, content, structure, or style.

Text-to-self connections occur when readers use something from their personal experience or memory to help them understand what is happening on the page. While reading "Valentine for Ernest Mann" I made a text-to-self connection when I remembered the Christmas my husband gave me a cappuccino maker. He had no idea he hurt my feelings. He thought I'd love having a new kitchen appliance. He didn't know I had put a great deal of thought and effort into his gift—a mountain bike—and had saved for months to buy it for him. I was also angry; I don't even drink coffee! Thinking about how I felt when I got this gift helped me understand why the woman in the poem cried when she got skunks.

I made another text-to-self connection with the line "Nothing was ugly just because the world said so." For years, I thought the black oil I saw on garage floors and in my mechanic's oil pan was the way oil was supposed to be, and I found the shiny, rich, black, gooey liquid beautiful. Finally an auto shop student told me that black oil was dirty oil and very harmful to a car's engine; to him, it was ugly.

Text-to-world connections are associations the reader makes between the text and his storehouse of knowledge about the world. They are factual and inform the reader about the workings of the past, present, and future. When I read the words "You can't order a poem like you order a taco" I thought of drive-thrus. I pictured how easy it is to place your order from your car, drive a short distance, and presto, there's dinner. Once again, I understood the poem more deeply: "writing poems is a lot harder than ordering food from a fast-food joint."

A text-to-text connection occurs when readers think about other written texts, such as movies, songs, or stories, to enhance their understanding of what they read. They may compare how two poems are structured, or they may consider similarities among authors or connections in subject matter. For example, before I started reading the Nye poem, I thought about the way in which poems are organized. I remembered that poets use visual images and metaphors in their writing and therefore looked for images and metaphors as I read. When Nye writes "And the poems that had been hiding in the eyes of skunks for centuries crawled out and curled up at his feet," I pictured the man staring at the skunk and realizing that beauty is in the eye of the beholder. I made a literal interpretation but was able to go beyond this and infer deeper meaning.

Connections help readers call on their background knowledge. When readers make connections to their reading, they have a richer experience. The more connections a reader makes to the text, the better her comprehension is.

But I Don't Have Any Connections: A Classroom Example

I've assigned "Man at the Well," a short vignette by Tim O'Brien about the Vietnam War to a reading workshop class, and they complain the piece is too hard: they weren't even alive when it happened. They think because they didn't experience it themselves, they can't understand it. I remind them that there are many topics they will have to read that didn't occur during the last fifteen years. It's time to show them how to call on the information they do have.

"Man at the Well" begins with an old blind Vietnamese farmer kindly administering to a few American soldiers who are returning from battle. Midway through the story, a large "blustery, stupid soldier" throws a milk carton at the old man, hitting him square in the face, causing his lip to bleed. The action freezes until the old man smiles and resumes drawing water from the well. The story ends, leaving the reader uneasy and a bit confused. It isn't necessary to know a lot about the Vietnam War in order to understand the vignette. Knowing about the war enhances one's understanding but is not crucial to it.

Niko claims, "I don't know anything about the Vietnam War."

"Nothing?" I ask skeptically. I suspect Niko knows more than he thinks. He is thinking too specifically about the Vietnam War. He needs to consider other topics related to the piece: the elderly, Asian cultures, cruelty, bullying, are all topics that will help Niko understand "Man at the Well" better.

How can I help him connect to "Man at the Well"? More important, how can I get him to use his background knowledge when I'm not around to do it for him? I tell the class, "When I don't know a lot about a topic I am reading, I think of other knowledge I have that might relate to the piece in some way. For example, thinking about war in general or the elderly or bullies would make 'Man at the Well' more familiar.

"How many of you know something about war? Think about movies, TV shows, other books you've read, or stories you've heard." Every student raises a hand. I record on the board what they know about wars. Some students talk about the Persian Gulf and a parent's involvement in it. Others share movie connections: *Full Metal Jacket* and *The Dirty Dozen*. These movies trigger still other students to recall television shows and documentaries they have watched. Several retell stories they have heard from grandparents and aunts and uncles.

I continue probing. "How many of you know something about bullies?" Once again, everyone raises a hand. We share aloud our experiences and memories about bullies who intimidated us or made us feel uncomfortable. The personal connections helped many students understand why the cruel American soldier hit the helpless old man.

Niko says, "At first I couldn't figure out why the American threw the milk carton at the old man. After thinking about war movies I've seen, I remembered how a lot of men during the Vietnam War became drug addicts and got really stressed out. Many of the soldiers were close to my age and probably didn't want to be there. I think the soldier hit the old man because he was angry and wanted to take it out on someone."

"Do you know what Niko just did?" I ask the class.

Surprised and a bit nervous he's done something wrong, he stares at me. I don't wait for an answer. I tell the class that Niko has just done something a good reader would do, and Niko smiles. I point out that his response shows that he has gone beyond the words and drawn an inference about the soldier's actions. He has used his background knowledge, put himself in the soldier's position, and was able to infer why the soldier threw the milk carton. "Niko couldn't have responded in this way if he were just reading the words. He had to connect the information in his head to the piece he was reading."

Now John offers a comparison. "The Vietnam War was similar to the American Civil War in that North and South Vietnam were fighting each other for political gain."

Ryan asks, "Why were we over there in the first place? It had nothing to do with us."

Kandice makes a strong visual connection to the piece. The images in a movie she's recently seen help her stay interested in the story: "I just kept seeing the soldiers in *Saving Private Ryan* and I didn't want to stop reading."

I don't want these real-world payoffs to go unnoticed. I point out that the connections the students are making allow them to read the piece more deeply. Niko draws an inference. John makes a comparison. Ryan asks a question. Kandice creates a strong visual image. Each of these thinking strategies help readers become better comprehenders of text.

So How Does It Help Me?

Eric is repeating reading workshop. He needs additional support reading expository text. One day, he scrunches up his forehead, raises his hand, and says, "Mrs. Tovani, all last year I wrote down my background knowledge and experiences all over my papers. I marked the text and made connections between my life and the book. I'm great at sharing my connections. The only problem is I have no idea why I am doing it. How does making connections between my life and the book help me become a better reader?"

Eric's question is a kind of epiphany. I have taught students how to make connections. They know how to mark these connections on their texts and how to use sticky notes to hold on to their thinking. Unfortunately, I've never taught them how it helps them as readers. Students are making connections to finish the assignment and get the grade. They aren't doing it to help them understand their reading better.

Realizing that I must teach readers to do more than just make connections, I begin to ask them how connections help them as readers. At first, they can't answer the question. They aren't sure how using their prior knowledge improves their ability to comprehend.

Looking to my own reading, I realize that some connections help me more than others. For example, if I read a piece about a dog and my connection is "This reminds me of my dog," I have not really helped myself understand the piece. But if I am more specific ("This reminds me of when my dog had surgery. She never came out of the anesthetic and died on the operating table. I wonder if this is going to happen to the dog in this story"), I have helped myself a lot. I have related to the character. I have asked a question and I have inferred a possible outcome. This one connection allows several other thinking processes to take place.

Initially, students' connections will be superficial, but with teacher modeling and practice they will become more sophisticated and will be able to go beyond the literal meaning on the page. Making connections helps readers:

1. *Relate to characters.* They understand how characters are feeling and the motivation behind their actions. Readers also learn about themselves and can ponder how they might react in a similar situation.

2. *Visualize.* They have a clearer picture in their head as they read. They are more engaged and thus have a tendency to continue reading.

3. *Avoid boredom.* They will be less likely to become bored while reading. The reading will be more enjoyable.

4. *Pay attention.* They have a purpose for reading, which keeps their mind from wandering.

5. *Listen to others.* They are curious to see how other readers are connecting to the text. They become more interested in others' opinions.

6. *Read actively.* They are forced to do more than "bark" at print. They become actively involved in the reading.

7. *Remember what they read.* They tend to remember what it is they are reading because the reading has become personalized.

8. *Ask questions.* Question often lead to inferences.

Connection Can Repair Confusion

Connections can help students repair confusion and read from a different perspective. One day my students are reading an entertaining rafting story by Pam Houston (1999), "A River Runs Through Them." In this piece, the author takes the reader on a six-day journey down a Utah river. As the students read the piece, I ask them to highlight parts in the text that confuse them. After reading several of the highlighted sections, I notice that in one particular spot many students have missed the author's attempt at humor and are confused.

In the passage in question, the author describes the city slickers' unwillingness to jump out of the raft to swim in the river: "Despite the heat, nobody will jump into the water on the first day. There are too many clothes to be taken off and put on, and they are afraid they'll look ungraceful trying to get back into the boat."

"This part is stupid, not funny," says Joey. "[The author] obviously doesn't know what she is talking about."

I explain that as an experienced river-rafting guide, Pam Houston probably does know what she is talking about.

"Well, the people in the boat are stupid then," he answers back. Not exactly the high-level response I was hoping for. However, it does provide an opportunity to show the class that sometimes a reader must read a piece from a different perspective, to infer how someone other than himself would react.

"Think about your mom or someone who lives in a city. Someone who is older than you. How would you think they would act in this situation?"

Joey smiles. "My mom would probably be afraid she'd ruin her hair. I bet she'd try to act like she really didn't want to go in the water even though she was hot. If she did go in the water, my dad would probably have to help her get back in the boat."

Next, I ask the class to think about a time in their life when they were embarrassed. How did they react? I read the funny part aloud again. Then I begin to think out loud, sharing something I remember from a vacation. I describe trying to hop on a raft floating in the pool, which turns out to be quite difficult. All day I have watched children jump and ride on rafts quite effortlessly; I wonder why I am having so much difficulty. I jump on the raft and it shoots out from under me. I look around hoping no one has noticed. I try again. No luck. Eventually I give up. Sparing myself further embarrassment, I get out of the pool.

Students shake their head and wonder how this is supposed to help them read the piece. I explain that thinking about this experience in the pool helps me understand why the rafters didn't want to jump into the river. They didn't want to embarrass themselves. I empathize. I understand the city slickers' motivation for not wanting to get wet. I, too, would be afraid of looking stupid reentering the boat. What if my derriere stuck up in the air as I tried to get back on board? Imagine my rear end up as my legs kick, struggling to climb into the raft. I can just see my husband telling me to quit fooling around.

As I describe what I'm thinking, I can see smiles spread across the faces of my students. They begin to see the humor. Sharing my connection helps them visualize what the writer is trying to convey. They understand the story better because they have read it from another perspective. They see reading come alive, that it is okay to find humor in a piece even if it is one they read at school. Modeling thinking out loud allows students to see how a reader can link experiences to the text in order to make it more interesting.

John wants to try it on his own. "This reminds me of the movie *A River Runs Through It*. Maybe this piece will be about fishing and families who come together. It might be a good story. I'm going to read it." John uses a movie connection to help him predict. Good readers are constantly making predictions and constantly confirming or disproving them. John makes another connection after reading "is it true that last year somebody died?" He writes, "This reminds me of stories my brothers told me when I was little. I would wonder if I should believe them or not. Maybe the stories of someone dying in the piece aren't true either." John's connection to his brothers' teasing helps him infer. He understands that maybe the stories referred to in the text are exaggerations and shouldn't be taken at face value.

In my classroom, identifying connections, asking questions, making inferences, drawing confusions, and describing strong visual images often replace tedious comprehension questions. Many students readily admit they can answer correctly many traditional comprehension questions without even reading the text. Likewise, students frequently joke about how they have bluffed their teachers when writing answers to short essay questions.

When readers have a means by which to hold on to their thinking, they are more willing to discuss what they read. Last fall I taught a graduate-level literacy course to preservice teachers. Some had already begun their internships, which meant they were designing and teaching units. I asked the class whether anyone had created a lesson that was a complete failure. Had they ever assigned reading to be discussed the following day only to return to a room full of zombies staring blankly at the floor? They laughed, but no one raised a hand. They thought I was crazy to suggest that their discussion questions would not provoke lively conversation. It was my turn to laugh. I knew they would all soon experience the zombie scenario.

When I first left elementary school to teach high school, I frequently stood in front of large classes of students sitting passively waiting for me to fill them up with knowledge. I had assumed that older students would be just as enthusiastic to share their thinking as the little ones. Wrong. I quickly learned that if I wanted students to participate in class discussions, I needed to give them a means by which they could connect and interact with the author. The easiest way to do this is to show students how to make connections to the text.

Sometimes readers initially complain that making connections interferes with their reading. This usually happens because students have never been asked to be aware of the thinking taking place inside their head. When meaning breaks down, readers need to know which strategies will enhance meaning and which ones won't. I give students many opportunities in class to practice making connections so that when they become confused when they are reading on their own, they can consciously apply the strategy to enhance comprehension.

What Works

1. Show students similarities between courses. Help them blur boundaries and encourage them to use the information they learn in one class to fortify their learning in another. Teach students to look for logical connections. Point out patterns among text structures, authors, genres, and factual information. Notice similarities in the way texts are organized. Recognize similarities in author style. Show traits common to specific genres. Let students see how different courses support their learning.

   TEACHING POINT: Good readers look for patterns in text, author style, genres, and other content areas in order to help them better understand new information.

2. Show students how to call up and use their background knowledge and experiences before, during, and after they read. First brainstorm collective knowledge as a class. Record connections on chart paper so readers can add to the list as they read. Then give students an opportunity

before they begin reading a piece to call up their own knowledge and experiences. Simply making the first question of an assignment *List everything you know about* _____ will encourage students to begin using this strategy on their own. Point out that students don't need a teacher to call up their background knowledge. Show them how you call up yours. Help students assume the responsibility of doing this on their own. Teach them to think about what they know about a topic before they begin reading.

TEACHING POINT: Good readers don't wait for others to call up their background knowledge. They know that using this information before, during, and after they read will enhance their understanding.

3. Provide examples of text-to-self, text-to-world, and text-to-text connections. Teach students that linking memories, experiences, factual knowledge, and other texts to their reading can help them stay interested. Model your thinking by sharing the connections you make while reading a text. Help students see how their life experiences enrich their reading.

TEACHING POINT: Good readers use many types of connections to help them relate and understand what they are reading. They recognize they have useful information in their head that can help them understand a piece of text.

4. Show students how thinking about topics in general terms when they don't have a lot of specific information can help them stay more engaged in the reading. Brainstorm possible topics students can think about to help them understand a piece.

TEACHING POINT: Good readers relate to topics any way they can. They use whatever knowledge they have about a piece to make sense of it. The more they read about a topic the greater their background knowledge will be.

5. Point out the real-world payoffs of making connections. Create a chart in the classroom so students can refer to it. Ask students how connections help them become better readers. Make sure they understand that a superficial connection doesn't necessarily mean they are understanding the text.

TEACHING POINT: Good readers appreciate the real-world payoffs of making connections. They know that background knowledge helps them relate to characters, visualize, avoid boredom, pay attention to the text, listen to others' responses, read actively, remember information, question the text, and infer answers.

6. Give students opportunities to practice making connections. Model your connections and give students time to do it on their own. Honor

their connections by sharing them and giving them credit for their attempts.

TEACHING POINT: Good readers record connections in order to hold on to their thinking, which can later be used to support points in a discussion or a writing assignment.

7   What Do You Wonder?

Real-world questions are things you really wonder about. They affect a lot of people. School questions are easy to answer and just affect people who don't understand what's going on.

Amanda, grade 12

I begin class one Monday morning with a seemingly simple question: "What do you wonder?"

"What do you mean, what do we wonder?" asks Ardis.

"What are you curious about? What questions do you have?" I say.

"Questions about what?" Ardis wants to know.

"Questions about anything," I continue.

"I don't wonder about nothin'."

"Oh, come on. You have to wonder about something. There are no right answers here. You can have questions about anything." Ardis crosses his arms and turns his back to me. "Okay, does anyone else have a question you don't know the answer to?" Eyes are averted, my plea ignored. I wait, calling their bluff.

Jim finally raises his hand. With relief, I call on him, hoping he will get the ball rolling. He smiles and says, "I wonder why we are doing this."

A few kids giggle. Most shrug their shoulders and mutter under their breath, "This is dumb." For the time being, they refuse to play.

For the last eight weeks, these reading workshop students have focused on learning how to call up and use background knowledge and experiences. They are successfully making connections between their lives and their reading. More important, they are integrating background knowledge with new information they encounter in print. Midterm exams are approaching and it seems fitting to introduce a new comprehension strategy, *self-questioning* the text. I know that promoting student-generated questions will lead to improved comprehension (Dole et al. 1991, p. 246). I further reason that if students can ask better questions, they may begin to think like the test maker and anticipate test items.

Believe it or not, I love teaching students how to ask questions. At first, they resist the urge to share their curiosities, fearing they will be laughed at or accused of being stupid. Yet I haven't taught a student yet who wasn't eventually successful at questioning the text.

I am, however, always disturbed by teenagers' initial lack of curiosity. In the beginning, students act as though they aren't inquisitive about anything.

Common sense tells me this can't be true. They may not wonder about politics or world affairs but surely they wonder about something: athletics, music, religion, sex. But they feign apathy so convincingly. Can they really be this detached? Was my middle school colleague correct when she said students lose their ability to ask questions when they turn thirteen?

Ten years of teaching elementary school haven't prepared me for such indifference. Elementary children question everything. Their enthusiasm for the unknown is boundless. Teenage apathy serves as a new roadblock to learning. Their refusal to nurture curiosity about anything school related seems peculiar to secondary students.

Who Is Really Doing the Work?

It is no wonder teachers of adolescents are frustrated when their students seem so disinterested in the amazing world around them. Teachers complain that poor readers, the ones who need to ask questions the most, don't.

It's tempting for teachers to take over, especially when faced with a classroom of unresponsive teenagers. When I taught elementary school, I spent hours creating comprehension questions about the novels we studied. I was doing the majority of the thinking and consequently receiving most of the benefits. Every Saturday, I would prepare for the following week by dissecting chapters, pulling out difficult vocabulary, and creating what I thought were wonderful, thought-provoking questions. I was careful to ask not only literal questions but also inferential ones. I reasoned that if students could complete my units, they understood what they were reading. I didn't realize how easy it was to fake an answer or copy from a friend.

I became a *Bloom's Taxonomy* disciple and expanded my questioning technique to include "cute" projects that went with his hierarchy of thinking. Eventually it dawned on me that asking high-level, thought-provoking questions didn't necessarily mean I would get high-level, thought-provoking answers. Most of the time, I received cursory answers that demonstrated superficial thinking.

It shouldn't have been surprising that students lost interest when my questions were the only ones getting answered. At the time, I didn't want to promote inquiry because unplanned questions from students caused me to stray from my lesson plans. I didn't know that if students generated their own questions not only would they remember the information better, they would be more interested in the reading. It became apparent that as long as my questions were the only ones that counted, I was going to be the only one interested in answering them.

In many traditional classrooms, the teacher is solely responsible for asking the questions, and eventually students become disenfranchised. Teachers easily assume the role of inquisitor, hurling question after question as they try to assess who read yesterday's assignment and who understands the material just introduced. Granted, there are times when it is important to know who has completed the homework. Teachers need to assess who is understanding and who is not in order to evaluate instruction and mastery.

But classroom inquiry cannot stop here. Often, only a handful of students participate in this rapid-fire questioning game. The rest opt out, especially in classrooms where students are only given the opportunity to ask questions about procedures and due dates. In a rigorous, inquiry-based classroom, student-generated questions drive instruction and encourage engagement.

Teachers who focus solely on covering large amounts of curriculum complain that they don't have time to let students ask questions. If teachers don't permit students to wonder, they restrict discovery. Forging paths of new thinking is discouraged when students aren't allowed to cultivate uncertainties. When readers are encouraged to ask questions, classrooms perk up and more than a handful of kids participate.

Real-World Questions

The good news is that questioning is a strategy that can be taught in connection with any subject, to students of all abilities. Readers who are taught how to question the text can infer and clear up confusion better than those who simply decode words and accept ideas unchallenged. At the start of any new comprehension strategy, it is crucial that the teacher provide authentic examples showing how the strategy works outside of school. In the real world, the learner, the one wanting information, initiates the questions. When I want to know something, I find a source that will help me. Sometimes it is a person. Sometimes it is a book. In either case, I initiate the questioning. When one question is answered, another one usually arises. The more I learn, the more sophisticated my questions become. Through questioning, I gain new information and I am better able to apply what I have learned.

When I wanted a new kitchen floor, I asked the contractor what would last longer, granite or slate? The contractor told me, and then I asked how much money each would cost. Through questioning, I learned enough to make an informed decision.

Often the learner asks a question of the expert and the expert has to ask the learner a question in order to give an answer. When I wanted to plant a new flower bed, I asked the man at the nursery what to plant. Before he could answer my question, he needed an answer to one of his: "How much sun does the plot get during the day?" Neither the contractor nor the nursery worker spouted information for me to follow blindly. Both the experts and I participated in the learning by virtue of the questions we asked.

Ardis didn't share his questions because he wasn't sure what I was asking him to do. He knew that in school the teacher was usually the one asking the questions. I had to show the class how to do it. Whenever an activity fails, it is because I haven't done enough modeling. Modeling gives students words and examples to frame their thinking. Since I wonder about the world around me constantly, it is easy to share real curiosities I have about everyday life. I brainstorm my questions in front of the class, recording the things I wonder about on the board. I use the words *I wonder* before each question I ask. Like this:

I wonder why Columbine happened. Why were the two gunmen so angry?

I wonder where the Anasazi people went. Are they today's Navajo?

I wonder how to access my school e-mail from home.

I wonder why the United States feels compelled to be the world's police force.

I wonder whether my oldest daughter will become a high school teacher.

The students are interested in my questions, and after this bit of modeling they realize they have questions too.

"Is that all you want us to do?" Katie asks. "I can do that."

"Sure you can," I tell her. "Did you notice that some of my questions don't have an answer and that some of them can only be answered with time?"

Before long students are eager to share what they are curious about. My faith is reaffirmed. Ardis, a streetwise kid who has experienced more violence in his short fifteen years than most adults do in a lifetime, peers out from under his Raiders' baseball cap and asks in a voice daring me to answer, "Why are blacks always killin' blacks?"

I respond by writing his question on a projected transparency. The room is silent as the class waits for my answer. I give none and wait for more "I wonders."

Tina breaks the silence with a completely different question: "How does aspirin know where to go?"

"Yeah, how does aspirin know where to go?" someone else repeats. A few kids, skilled at playing the game of school, begin to answer Tina's question. I stop and remind them that today we are concentrating on asking questions, not answering them.

Charlotte, a withdrawn student, surprises us, breaking her usual shell of silence. "Why do some people in my family do drugs?" The class respects her question and doesn't try to answer it. The attention is diverted from Charlotte when Andy wonders why there are so few places to Rollerblade.

Dean wonders why fireflies glow. Roy wants to know what happens when you die.

Frank asks, "How come time goes fast when you are having fun and slow when you are bored?" I write as quickly as I can: recording their questions validates their thinking. It becomes obvious that there are no wrong answers and that every question is valid.

Author and poet Georgia Heard teaches that questions are the seeds of powerful poetry. Experimenting with this idea, I ask the students to rewrite their questions as poems. Even though some students are intimidated by poetry, they give it a try. I model the assignment, playing with white space and arranging my questions into a poem. I leave out some and add a few more. As I work on my "poem," the class eagerly works on theirs.

Making poems out of authentic questions is intellectually elevating. "I wonder" poems dignify inquiry and validate personal curiosities. Often they are quite beautiful and serve as powerful reminders to teachers and students alike that school is a place to honor and celebrate questions.

The next day, students eagerly recopy their poems on colored paper. As they finish, I post them around the entrance to the classroom. In large letters above the door hangs a sign that says *What Do You Wonder?*

"I Wonder"

Why do people treat other people by the way they dress?
Why does God make people different colors?
Why do people act like your friend when they aren't?
Why does my cousin live the way he does?
Why did God make me the way I am?
    by Tiffany

"I Wonder"

Where does space end
and what's after that?
What's after eternity?
Where is heaven and hell?
Who made God?
    by Shannan

On to the Text

Once students have begun to ask questions about the world around them, it's time to teach them how to begin asking questions about text. Following the gradual-release-of-responsibility model (Pearson and Gallagher 1983), I initially assume the principal role in the learning process. For the time being, I do most of the work as I model how I ask questions when I read. Gradually I will turn the responsibility for the question asking over to the students. For now, I must show them how I question a piece of text.

I choose something that I am actually reading, an article from the newspaper about a seventy-two-year-old elephant that has starved herself to death, grieving for a companion. I copy the article on a transparency and project it so students can follow along as I read aloud. I begin reading and almost immediately stop. I look up from the text and share aloud the question that has popped into my head as I write it on the projected transparency: "I wonder if the elephant really did die of a broken heart." I don't answer the question: it's been recorded on the transparency, and I will return to it later to see where the answer can be found. For right now, the focus of this lesson is to model how to ask questions, not answer them. I continue reading aloud, stopping whenever a question arises: "I wonder if it's possible for an animal to care so much for another animal that she dies of grief." "I wonder where this elephant died. In the zoo? the wild?"

Each time I ask a question, I put the words *I wonder* in front of it. These two words help students frame their curiosity as a question and lead them toward inferential thinking. At first, students tend to make predictions instead of asking questions. Adding *I wonder* to a statement changes a prediction into a question and allows the reader to go beyond the text, which in turn makes inferential thinking possible.

Most adolescents are capable of making logical predictions. Predictions are either correct or incorrect. Inferential thinking isn't directly confirmed by the author, and therefore it is more difficult to do. If a reader is able to question the text, he or she is more inclined to draw conclusions when his questions aren't directly answered in what is read.

Sometimes a reader must go to another source to find the answer to his or her question. I go back to reading the article about the grieving elephant and have two additional questions: *What happens to elephants in the wild when a poacher kills a member of their group? Do elephants really recognize the bones of dead relatives?* These questions aren't answered in the text and can't be answered by drawing an inference. There is nothing in the story that mentions poachers or the bones of dead relatives. In order to find answers, I must go to another source.

I record these last two questions and pause in order to give the class a chance to share theirs. They stare at the overhead, and then back at me wondering why I am reading them an article about elephants in a reading workshop class. They don't see the connection between being curious about the world around them and being curious about what they read. More important, they don't understand the need to transfer their knowledge about questioning the world to questioning the text. I remind them of the important questions they asked in their "I wonder" poems and I tell them that now we are trying to learn how to ask questions when we read. The bell rings. On her way out, Theresa says, "I don't wonder about anything when I read."

"Don't worry," I answer. "You will."

Good Readers Ask Questions All the Time

Good readers constantly question the text. They ask questions before, while, and after they read. After reading only the title of the elephant article ("Grieving Elephant Starves Self to Death in Zoo"), I wonder about the details surrounding the elephant's death. How old was she? Is it possible she really died because of old age or because she was sick? These questions asked early on give me a purpose for reading the article. I want to find the answers.

Questioning engages readers especially in relation to difficult or uninteresting material. If readers look for answers to their questions, they focus on the text and their mind is less inclined to wander. Asking questions gives reticent and struggling readers control over their learning.

Good readers also ask questions while they are reading. Sometimes their questions clarify information that was missed on the first reading. For instance, one of the things I wanted to know was where the elephant died. The title clearly states it was in a zoo, but I missed it the first time around.

The more-complex questions that arise aren't as easily answered. When I read fiction, I wonder what will happen to a character. I wonder whether there is meaning or symbolism in an object that keeps reappearing in the story. When I read nonfiction, I wonder how something works or why something happens. Questions encourage reading.

Good readers often still have questions when they finish reading. These questions tend to be ponderable and don't have simple answers. Sometimes they require the reader to go beyond the text and infer. They may even require the reader to go to another source in order to find the answer. Questions asked after the reading tend to encourage more thinking and deeper analysis of the material. For some students having a question other than *What did this piece mean?* after finishing a piece is a new concept. "The end" is really just the beginning.

Why Teach Questioning?

Readers who ask questions when they read assume responsibility for their learning and improve their comprehension in four ways:

1. *By interacting with text.* Students who are assigned difficult nonfiction often grumble that their mind wanders and they don't remember what they read. Readers who intentionally ask questions establish a purpose for their reading and tend to be more focused. Students are more invested in the material because they own their questions. Questioning forces students to attend to print.

2. *By motivating themselves to read.* Readers who are taught how to question a text are more likely to grapple with meaning in order to find the answers to their questions. Questioning fosters curiosity and encourages the reader to stay with the material. Readers who ask questions are propelled to read on as they look for the answers to their questions; they find what they are reading interesting.

3. *By clarifying information in the text.* Clarifying questions ask who, what, why, when, and where. They help the reader understand elements of plot, character, and setting. They also elucidate directions, concepts, and processes. In order to think more deeply about a text, readers must clarify simple confusions and fill in missing information. Readers who ask clarifying questions are not necessarily literal thinkers. They may be verifying basic information in order to comprehend the text more fully. Clarifying questions may indicate that a reader needs more support in order to clear up confusion. Answers to clarifying questions are usually found in the text quickly and easily.

4. *By inferring beyond the literal meaning.* Teachers often lament that their students don't infer. It's difficult to infer without first wondering about something. Expecting students to infer before they question a text is unreasonable. Inferential thinking is born out of questions the reader has about information stated indirectly in the text. Inferences are found in the reader's head. They are not directly stated in the text but rather deduced from clues left by the author, combined with the reader's background knowledge. Questioning helps readers go beyond literal meaning in order to engage in inferential thinking.

Guiding Their Practice

After sufficient modeling of *how* I ask questions, I give students an opportunity to try it with some guided practice. I select an article from *The Washington Post*. The story reports that eleven children have mistreated and killed a horse apparently for no reason. The wanton violence described in the story is sickening. Several students in the class have recently demonstrated cruelty toward a classmate. In addition to wanting my students to practice questioning, I am curious to see how they will react to the story about the horse. Will they recognize the children's actions as being cruel or will they think the torture was amusing?

I make a copy of the article for each student and a transparency of it to project on the overhead. I announce that I found a disturbing story in the newspaper and I have a lot of questions about it. I ask them to read the article and record their questions in the margins next to the words that have caused them to wonder. (Recording their questions in the margins helps them remember what they were thinking when they read.) I tell them that after everyone has finished we'll discuss their thinking.

Everyone begins reading the piece and marking the text. I record my questions on the overhead transparency as students record theirs on their copy. Occasionally, I glance around the room, looking for reactions. I notice that several students are reading but not writing. Others are making faces as they read. After a few minutes comments begin erupting everywhere.

"This is sick. Why would kids put a stick up a horse's nose?"

"Yeah, I wondered that too," I say. "Write that question in the margin so you won't forget it."

"Do we have to answer our questions?" asks Miquel. "Because if we do, I don't have any." Miquel knows how to play the game of school and is afraid there will be more work if he isn't careful.

I reassure Miquel that he won't have to answer his questions and tell him that sometimes questions are more powerful than answers. Students continue reading and marking thoughts down in the margins. As I weave through the room looking over shoulders, I am amazed by the questions I see. Soon it's time for them to share their thinking so they can benefit from one another's questions. "Okay, tell us some of your questions. I'll record them on a blank transparency."

Samantha asks, "Were the kids in the story abused?"

"What kind of family life did the kids have?" Kimberly wants to know.

When John begins to answer her, I put up my hand. "Right now, we're concerned about asking questions, not answering them. Let's just try to get what we're wondering down on the transparency; we'll worry about answering our questions later."

Without missing a beat, Miquel jumps in. "Why would these kids think it was cool to be arrested?"

"I think they want attention," said Jeremy.

"Jeremy, you just gave us a prediction. Can you restate your prediction as a question?" I ask. Jeremy taps his head and thinks for a minute.

"How about," he begins, "I wonder if the kids wanted attention?"

"Great job, Jeremy."

"I wonder if they hurt the horse in retaliation for something the owner did," said Lindsay.

Wanting to join the group, Jim raises his hand and says, "Were the kids cruel?"

I study Jim's face, trying to decipher whether he is being silly or is having trouble understanding the strategy. "Jim, do you know the answer to that question?"

"Sure, of course the children were cruel."

Now is the perfect time, so I say it: "There is such a thing as a dumb question. A dumb question is one that you already know the answer to. Why ask it? It's a waste of time."

"Teachers do it constantly," Jim smiles. "They always ask questions they know the answers to."

He's right. I get a bit defensive and feel I owe it to my profession to explain. "Well, Jim, you're right. Teachers do this because they want to check for understanding." Jim's comment reminds me how well some students play the game of school. It also makes me wonder how much thinking students are doing if answers are so quickly and simplistically returned. I ask Jim to try again. "This time ask a question you really wonder about."

Jim thinks and after a bit says, "What would these kids do to a child if they did this to an animal?"

"Good question," I nod. The room is quiet as students ponder Jim's question.

I am amazed by their thinking and relieved that they identify the cruelty. I record their questions for the entire period. Recording what they are wondering validates their ideas and provides an opportunity to revisit their thinking later.

The following day, we pick up where we left off. I put the transparency back on the overhead and continue recording questions. When we finish there are three transparencies full of questions and only one of the fifty is a clarifying question. All the others require the reader to go to another source. I tell the students that often the answers to a reader's questions aren't found in the text or in the reader's head.

Although the class has done well asking questions about the tortured-horse article, they still need more guided practice before I can expect them to do it on their own. I give them another opportunity to practice, this time using the novel *I Had Seen Castles,* by Cynthia Rylant (1993). The story is a flashback told by a World War II soldier and can be confusing if students don't clarify what is happening early in the book.

First I demonstrate the importance of asking questions before beginning to read a novel. I give a copy to each student and ask them to look at the cover and flip through the chapters. I encourage them to read the back and a paragraph here and there inside. As they preview, I ask them to think about questions they have. Attached to the chalkboard is a piece of chart paper headed *Good Readers Ask Questions Before Reading.* I begin recording the "before" questions they have about the book:

Where is the story taking place?

Is a war going on? What war? Who is fighting?

Who is on the cover?

Is this a love story?

Is there a storm during which people die?

Is this about someone in the author's life?

Will it end happily?

What do castles have to do with the story?

Looking at the list of questions, I point out which ones are likely to be answered in the text and which ones will probably have to be answered by drawing an inference. We discuss which questions will help us better understand what's happening and which ones are unimportant to the story. I also wonder aloud which questions a teacher might ask, helping them anticipate what might appear on an exam. I point out that good readers have lots of questions at the beginning of a novel. If authors told readers everything on the jacket flap or the back cover, there would be no reason to read the book. The author slowly reveals information, allowing readers to answer their own questions.

I start reading the first chapter aloud and almost immediately stop because I have a question. Since my students aren't allowed to write in their books, I head to the supply cabinet and pull out several packages of sticky notes. I toss them around the room and say, "When you can't write in your books, you can use these to help record your thinking." I instruct everyone to take at least three sticky notes and then model how to use them. I share my question, and write it on a sticky note, making sure to explain where to put it. I demonstrate how to attach the note in the margin so it is visible when the book is closed. (This saves time when you wish to go back to something.) I then say, "Put the sticky note as close as you can to the words that caused your question and make sure to write the question and the page number on the sticky note." I continue reading and questioning. Occasionally, I stop and ask, "Is anyone wondering anything?"

"I'm wondering," Theresa asks, "who is talking right now. The boy or the man?"

"Write that question down on one of your stickies and put it on the page where you are wondering."

After a few more pages and a few more of my questions I tell the class it's their turn. "Read the rest of the period and record three of your questions on sticky notes."

While the students read, I circle around the room, stopping to talk to students who seem stuck. Paul says, "I don't wonder anything." I read the part he just read and model a question I have. Then I ask him to read the next paragraph aloud and share what he is wondering. He does and says, "Nothing." It's a very straightforward paragraph, so I agree: "I don't wonder anything here either. Let's keep reading." He reads the next paragraph. This time he does have a question. Since it's one he doesn't know the answer to, I praise his thinking. When class is over, I collect the books and examine all the questions.

I copy each question from a sticky note onto two note cards, once in red ink, then again in blue. I record the name of the person who asked the question on the bottom of each card. Next, I attach five sheets of chart paper to the chalkboard and write a heading at the top of each one. The first three headings are written with a red marker: *In the Text, In My Head,* and *In Another Source.* The fourth—*Ponderable Questions*—and fifth—*Clarifying Questions*—are written with a blue marker.

When the students return to class the next day, I hand each person a note card. I introduce the charts and explain that they are going to analyze the questions from the previous day. I ask for a volunteer and Brandon reads his: "'Is the person telling the story old or young?'"

I ask Brandon if his question is written in red or blue ink. He tells me, "Red." I direct Brandon's attention to the three charts with red headings—*In the Text, In My Head,* and *In Another Source*—and ask him to decide where he thinks the answer to his question might be found.

After some help from the class, he decides that the answer to his question would probably be found in the book if he kept reading. I ask Brandon to tape his note card to the chart that says *In the Text.* Then I ask, "Who has the same question written in blue ink?"

Katie raises her hand. "I do."

"Katie, can you figure out if your question is a clarifying question or a ponderable question."

"What's a ponderable question?" she asks.

"A ponderable question is one that doesn't have a simple answer. Sometimes it doesn't have an answer at all. For example, *What is the meaning of life?* That's a ponderable question."

"Hmm," she pauses. "I think this is a clarifying question and that Brandon is right. If we keep reading, it will become clear who is speaking." Katie takes her blue question and tapes it to the chart headed *Clarifying Questions.*

I am pleased with Brandon's and Katie's thinking. It's time to move on. I see that Ardis is holding a red card. "Read your question, Ardis."

Ardis reads, "What does the author mean when she says, 'Breakfast is the finest hour'?"

"Where do you think the answer to that question can be found?" I ask.

Immediately he says, "In the text."

I ask the class to turn to page 9, the page the quote was taken from, and ask them to look for the answer. Of course no one finds it. Ardis is frustrated.

"Look at the other two choices, *In My Head* and *In Another Source.*"

"No research book or dictionary is gonna help me," he says. I remind Ardis that another source can also be an expert on the subject. Still convinced that using another source won't help him, he chooses *In My Head* by default: "I guess my only choice is *In My Head,* but what does that mean?"

"It means that you have to use your background knowledge in addition to the clues from the text to answer the question. Unfortunately, since we are only on page 9, we don't have a lot of textual clues to help us. Do you think you could answer this question with the knowledge you have in your head?"

"Probably," Ardis says. "I guess this guy really likes breakfast, and that's why he thinks it is the finest hour of the day."

"That makes sense to me," I say.

Ardis strolls to the chalkboard with his card. "This question belongs on the *In My Head* chart."

"I have the same question in blue," says Justine, "and I don't think it is a ponderable question. So I am going to put it on the clarifying sheet."

Hoping to find a question that has to be answered with another source, I ask if anyone thinks they have one.

Dimario raises his hand. "I do. My question is, 'What is a uranium atom?'"

"Why do you think that is an *In Another Source* question?"

"Because it doesn't tell us in the text what it is. I get the feeling that the author thinks we already know what a uranium atom is, but I don't have a clue. I'd have to go to another source to find the answer."

I ask the class if they agree or disagree with Dimario.

"I disagree," says Slava. "I know what a uranium atom is. The information is in my head. So that question for me would be an *In Your Head* question."

"If that's true, Slava, you wouldn't have asked the question in the first place." I remind the class that good readers don't ask questions they already know the answer to. "The book doesn't tell the reader what a uranium atom is, and Dimario can't make an inference because he doesn't have the information in his head. The only option for him is to check another source." Not waiting for approval, Dimario tapes his question to the *In Another Source* chart.

Theresa has the same question in blue and decides that it too is a clarifying question. The class begins to notice that they asked a lot more clarifying questions than ponderable ones. I explain that when a reader first begins a book or an article, he has more clarifying questions because, if it's fiction, he's trying to establish plot, and if it's nonfiction, he's trying to figure out what is happening. I remind the class of the advantage they have when they get an opportunity to reread something. Clarifying questions are often answered on the first read. On the second read the reader can focus on more ponderable questions.

John, concerned that all this question asking is a waste of time, wonders, "Why ask questions if you don't try to answer them?" He has a point. Asking questions for the sake of asking questions is a waste of time. The first goal in teaching the strategy of questioning is to help students ask questions. The second goal is to help them find the answers. When students are constantly fed information, they aren't allowed to participate in their learning. Questioning requires readers to think and actively engage in the reading.

"John," I ask, "have you ever taken a test and come upon a question you didn't know the answer to?"

"Sure, all the time," he says a little sheepishly.

"Would you have liked to have known where the answers were?"

"Yeah…" His tone indicates he is losing patience.

"Lots of times, the answer is in the student's head and he doesn't even realize it."

"What do you mean?"

I ask the class if they remember taking tests in elementary school, the ones where everyone had to fill in little circles. Most of them do and say how much they dreaded them. "I remember giving those tests," I say. "And I recall a question that always tricked my students."

"What was it?" John is eager to know.

"It was 'Pick the best title for this story.'"

"Oh, I hated those," moans Samantha.

"Me too," says John.

"The funny thing about that question," I say, "is that the kids reread the story looking for the answer."

"But the answer wasn't there," says John.

"That's right. Where was it?"

John smiles, "It was in their heads."

"Exactly," I continue. "If they had known the answer was in their heads, they wouldn't have reread the piece looking for it. By rereading the selection looking for an answer that wasn't there, they wasted valuable time. If a reader knows that the answer to his question can be found in his head, he can consciously stop and think about making an inference. Furthermore, when a reader knows the information is in another source, he doesn't waste time looking for it in the text."

Several students admit they never realized they could tackle questions by going to their head for answers. I reassure them that indeed, they often need to go beyond the words and supply their own thinking.

When a reader is passionate about something that interests him or her, it is easy to ask questions. Reading material that the reader values and wants to understand encourages questions. However, when adolescents encounter a subject area or a piece of reading material that doesn't particularly interest them, they have difficulty asking questions other than *What does this mean?* Their questions are general and not very passionate. Many fear that because the material is new, their questions may seem silly.

Teachers have a choice. We can choose to cover the curriculum or we can choose to teach students to inquire. If we choose to cover the curriculum, our students will fail. If we teach our students to inquire, we will have a well of information from which to teach and our students will have a purpose for learning. It is our obligation to renew our students' curiosity and guide them toward inquiry.

I would wager that there are very few successful people who don't ask questions. Most successful business people, attorneys, doctors, artists, and mechanics ask questions. As a reading teacher, it is difficult for me to get students to ask questions about physics and chemistry. I know so little about these subjects that it is hard for me to be interested in them. But I know that there are physicists and chemists in classrooms who, when they model their questions, spark the interest of their students and generate curiosity.

If teachers model their own questions and demonstrate the power of inquiry, students will be invested in the course. Too many students come to class merely to watch. They sit passively in their seats and wait for the teacher to fill them up with knowledge. Let students in on this important work. Teach them to question.

■ ■ ■ ■ ■ ■   *What Works*

1. Connect how questioning applies to the real world. Think about a hobby or a time when you needed to learn something. Try to remember some of the questions you asked and share them with your students. Point out how asking these questions helped you. Connect real-world experiences with reading and remind students that questioning the text improves comprehension. Recall questions you had the first time you read something and share these questions with your students. Provide opportunities for students to practice asking questions with material they read in class. Remind them that asking questions is an effective way to clear confusion.

TEACHING POINT: Good readers ask questions when they learn something new or read something unfamiliar. Asking questions facilitates learning and new information often leads to more sophisticated questions.

2. Create "I wonder" poems. They are a great way to introduce a unit and find out what background knowledge students have about a topic. They also encourage students to ask questions.

TEACHING POINT: Good readers are curious about the world around them. Asking questions and wanting more information gives them a reason to read.

3. Demonstrate that good readers ask questions throughout the reading process: before, during, and after reading. Use different pieces of text over several class periods to model how to ask authentic questions. Show how you would ask questions at various points while reading. For example, before starting a chapter, brainstorm on the chalkboard questions you have about the text. Model questions you had as you read the material. This is a good time to anticipate where students might have difficulty. Ask questions they might have. And model lingering questions, the ones that are left after you finish the text. Point out that these questions often don't have simple answers. Take time to make sure students "see" how you question the text. The first demonstration usually takes a class period. Subsequent demonstrations can be as short as two or three minutes. Select short pieces of text—poems, newspaper articles, snippets from a textbook—that invite curiosity. Model how to ask questions and eventually turn this task over to the students.

TEACHING POINT: Good readers ask questions before, during, and after they read.

4. Teach students that answers to their questions can be found in three places: in the text, in their head, and in another source. Give examples of each.

TEACHING POINT: Good readers know that sometimes answers to their questions aren't in the text and they need to go to other sources to find the answers.

5. Teach students how to mark text with their questions. Show them how to use sticky notes in case they can't write in their books.

TEACHING POINT: Good readers mark text to hold their questions so they can return to them later as they search for the answers. Marking questions also helps readers establish a purpose so their minds don't wander as they read.

8 Outlandish Responses: Taking Inferences Too Far

That's it? That's how the book ends? I don't even know what happened.

Kadee, grade 9

It's My Opinion

I've just finished reading aloud *I Never Knew Your Name*, by Sherry Garland (1994). An exasperated Kadee slams her hand on the desk and says, "I hate books that don't tell you how they end." Disgusted, she concludes that books without obvious endings are just plain bad. But there are conspicuous clues throughout this story that the teenage protagonist commits suicide by jumping off the roof of his apartment building. Kadee has missed important indicators that would help her infer the ending.

I decide to see who else in the class is unsure about what happened. I ask everyone to jot down on a sticky note how they think the book ended. A few immediately call out, "The boy dies." Others look up and then scribble their classmates' conclusion. Fairly certain that most students know the boy committed suicide, I begin recording their responses on the board. Much to my surprise, I get a variety of endings, many of them quite outlandish.

Tyler begins. "The boy moved."

"No, this book is about some kid who plays with pigeons on the roof of his apartment building," argues Tim. "One day for no reason he stops going up there."

Kristi is sure he overdosed on drugs.

Ratiba disagrees. "No, he didn't. He was shot."

Sampson agrees with Ratiba. "Yeah, someone shot him."

"I think he got hit by a car," Corey mutters under his breath.

Keyan calls out, "I think a crazed janitor pushed him off the roof." Everyone stops and looks at Keyan to see whether he is fooling around. When they realize he isn't, they assume they've missed something along the way. They know that Keyan's not kidding, but they don't know his conclusion is way off base. Keyan has taken inferring too far.

Intrigued by their responses, I wonder how they arrived at their conclusions. I ask whether they have any evidence from the text to support their thinking.

"What do you mean?" asks Kristi.

"Authors," I say, "leave clues in the text for the reader to find. They can't just make up endings without giving the reader some indication of what's going to happen. Good readers look for these clues as they read."

Kristi thinks. Then she says, "No, there isn't anything that tells me what happens. It's my opinion that the kid overdosed, and if it's an opinion, then it can't be wrong."

"Opinions are very important," I say, "but as you get older, people won't take you seriously if your opinions aren't based on the facts. You can't just say anything and expect people to agree with you. I have a responsibility to teach you how to substantiate your thinking. In school, ideas need to be bolstered by facts and information."

I explain to Kristi that the author has given the reader hints about the ending. I hand her the book and ask her to search the text for any evidence that might support her version of the ending. After a few minutes, she returns the book and admits that she can't find anything that confirms that the boy overdosed on drugs. Undaunted, she smiles and says, "It doesn't matter. It still could have happened."

"What do you mean, it could have happened?" I ask.

"Last year, my friend committed suicide by overdosing on her mother's pills. Who's to say that that didn't happen to the boy in the story?"

Students like Kristi don't expect reading to make sense. They cling desperately to plot and personal experiences, and when that doesn't yield meaning they make outlandish inferences. When Kristi's version of the story doesn't match mine, she releases herself of responsibility by saying, "It's my opinion." She doesn't understand that meaning, analysis, and interpretation aren't the whim of whoever is doing the reading. Many struggling readers don't appreciate their responsibility to draw conclusions and apply logical thinking. Good readers know that in order to understand a text more deeply they must collaborate with the author, searching for clues as they read and combining textual information with their background knowledge. The idea that readers can figure out the ending of a story logically is a foreign notion to readers like Kristi.

When Teaching the *What,* Don't Forget the *How*

By the time students enter middle school, they have begun to rely on their teachers to tell them what their reading is about. Teachers obligingly share their conclusions, assuming that that's the only way some students are ever going to "get it." In fourth grade, I asked my teacher to show me how she figured out a difficult ending. She smiled and said, "Cris, you need to read between the lines." I skipped happily back to my seat, thinking I had been given privileged information. I opened my book only to find to my disappointment that between the lines was just white space.

When teachers use phrases like *read between the lines, make an inference, draw a conclusion, think harder,* they are not showing students *how* to infer, they are merely *telling* them to infer. When students aren't taught how to "read between the lines," they begin to rely too heavily on their background knowledge or they simply guess. Perhaps this is why many students come up with outlandish conclusions when asked to think beyond the words.

Students who ignore textual evidence tend to rely solely on personal experience. A reader's background knowledge plays a significant role in her or his ability to infer. However, background knowledge alone is not enough. Readers must also use the text to support their thinking. Claiming "it's my opinion" doesn't automatically make the thinking correct or acceptable.

To demonstrate how I figure out endings, I take the book back from Kristi and show the class how I arrive at my version of the ending. I start at the beginning. I point out clues all the way through: the boy is always playing basketball by himself; he is sitting on the curb watching all the other kids go to the prom; he is often alone on the roof feeding the pigeons. The last time we encounter him, he is crying. I show the illustration depicting the ambulance's flashing lights. I show the picture of the shocked bystanders and share the words of a fellow student: "You weren't so bad. I wonder why you did it?"

Next, I use my background knowledge and experiences to make sense of the clues I have just described. "All of the information I just shared tells me that the boy in this story is lonely and that he doesn't have a lot of friends. In my experience, people who are often alone and depressed sometimes commit suicide. I think this boy ended his life by jumping off the roof." Students begin to see that my inference is based on textual evidence, not random guessing. Kristi again mentions the loss of her friend to a drug overdose: "People commit suicide when they are lonesome or feeling hopeless," she says. We recall several scenes in the book in which the author specifically mentions the boy's isolation.

"I agree," Jenny says. "The author is giving us clues that the boy is depressed and lonesome."

Corey remembers that the boy is always on the roof feeding pigeons. "I think he jumps. Why else would the author keep mentioning the roof?"

Others agree and by the time class ends, most of them, including Kristi, agree the boy commits suicide by jumping off the roof.

Encouraging Probable Outcomes

It is important not to appear to advocate outlandish conclusions by accepting all responses. As an elementary teacher, I unknowingly did this for fear of squelching children's enthusiasm. Students would share their thinking and because I was afraid I'd injure their self-esteem, I'd praise it no matter how ridiculous. I mistakenly figured that a bad response was better than no response. Instead of drawing students closer to meaning, I pulled them away from it.

Each day readers add to their store of background knowledge. New experiences allow them to bring fresh meaning to text each time it is read. Several years ago, I attended a workshop given by Donald Graves. Graves shared a habit of his that I've never forgotten. He admitted that he rereads *Anna Karenina* (Tolstoy 1889) every year and that each time he does, he finds something new in the book and in turn learns something new about himself. It was apparent that he relished the idea of drawing new meaning from a text that never changed: how disappointing it would be if the time ever came when he didn't discover something new about himself or the world after rereading *Anna Karenina*!

Bound by Words

Teachers often complain that students are bound by plot and that if they could infer, teaching would be so much easier. Inferring requires that the reader use an appropriate amount of background knowledge in combination with textual evidence. In *Mosaic of Thought,* Keene and Zimmermann (1997) write, "In order to infer, readers must lift up the words and go beneath them." As a teenage reader, I was confined by words. In English class, I found myself wondering how my teachers arrived at the conclusions they did. I didn't know how to think beyond the pages in order to find deeper meaning. I was restricted by the words. I didn't look for clues in the text, and I certainly didn't think my background knowledge was important.

I was never taught how to analyze a piece of writing. I was just told to do it. When I interpreted the material incorrectly, I'd chalk it up to another unintelligible piece of literature. I didn't know how the teacher was always able to get the "hidden meaning." I comforted myself by thinking that only English teachers and nerds needed such worthless information. Deep inside, though, I desperately wanted the keys to unlock the door to inferential thinking.

What Exactly Is an Inference?

Many adults have a difficult time explaining what an inference is. Teachers know this is a complicated strategy to teach. Inferring is abstract thinking, something readers do in their head when they are reading beyond the words. Harvey and Goudvis, authors of *Strategies That Work* (2000), tell readers that "inferring is the bedrock of comprehension."

When struggling readers are asked inferential questions, they have a tendency to return to the text, hoping to find the answer directly stated. They search in vain, not sure how much thinking they need to supply. They don't understand that authors cannot possible furnish every detail for the reader. If they did, books would be unwieldy and readers would lose the joy of participating.

Kristi and the rest of the class aren't sure what an inference is, let alone how to make one. I want to move them away from the idea that an opinion is just as good as an inference. Before I can teach the class how to infer, I need to help them understand what an inference is.

I start off by explaining that there is a place for opinions, but opinions are very different from inferences. "Opinions can be right or wrong," I say. "In my opinion, my brothers were the best baseball players in the state. The college and pro scouts that came to the practices and games thought differently, but I didn't care. My mind was set. My brothers were the best. This was my opinion and nothing was going to change it. My thinking was based on loyalty to my brothers, not logic. Inferences differ from opinions in that inferences are steeped in evidence and saturated in personal experience. Inferences are logical conclusions made with the mind, not the heart."

Philip, still unsure about the actual meaning of an inference, wants more clarification.

"An inference," I begin, "is a logical conclusion not directly confirmed by the author. It is based on clues from the text and personal connections made by the reader. Inferences are sometimes hard to make because the author doesn't come right out and confirm the reader's conclusions." Feeling completely satisfied with my definition, I survey the room, only to confront forty glazed eyes, fifteen slightly agape mouths, and three heads resting on desks.

Kelly speaks up, "I still don't get what an inference is."

"Me either," says Charity. "Why do some stories just end?"

Their questions don't have simple answers. I can't placate their frustration with a neat one-word solution.

Practice, Practice, Practice

When I teach readers how to apply a new comprehension strategy to their own reading, I show them how to do it in simple steps. First, I help them recognize what the strategy is. Second, I create situations in which they have an opportunity to experience what it is like to use the strategy correctly. Third, I support their attempts to implement the strategy on their own. Fourth, I give them time to practice the strategy on ever more difficult material.

Athletes often follow these same steps when perfecting their game. For example, when I first began teaching my daughter Rhiannon how to play tennis, I stood next to her and gently dropped a ball in front of her for her to hit. When she was able to hit the ball successfully, I made the task more difficult. I gradually moved farther away until I had crossed the net. Eventually I picked up a racquet myself and we began hitting the ball back and forth over the net. All the while, I gave her encouragement and instruction about how to hit a proper forehand. If I had begun by standing at the opposite baseline and blasting balls across the net, Rhiannon would have given up and concluded that she wasn't a good tennis player.

Sometimes we ask our students to be proficient at a task before they have had any practice. It is unrealistic to ask readers to draw conclusions from difficult text without first showing them how.

Seen and Unseen Text

To make my students aware of what it is like to infer, I read a story by James Marshall (1976) from his children's series about two charming hippos named George and Martha. The books consist of several short vignettes that usually teach a lesson. My favorite, "The Scary Movie," begins with George inviting Martha to a horror picture. Martha hesitates because she's never been to one before and is worried she'll be frightened. George reassures her that "everyone likes scary movies," so Martha agrees to go. But it is George, not Martha, who becomes frightened. He is seen bending down, claiming to look for his glasses, when actually he is hiding his eyes. Martha bluntly reminds him that he doesn't wear glasses. After the movie, as the two walk home, George is as white as a sheet. He insists on holding Martha's hand so she "won't be frightened." Martha smiles and tells George how much she enjoyed the movie.

After I finish, I ask the class what happened. Everyone realizes that George is the one who is scared and that he is trying to cover up his embarrassment. I ask how they know that George is frightened. I remind them that the author never comes out and says "George is scared" but that somehow they all know he is.

"It's obvious," says Kristi. "George is pretending to look for his glasses when he is really hiding his eyes."

"Why do you think that?" I ask.

"When I'm with my friends and I'm scared, I make up excuses so I miss the bad parts. I don't want them to know that I'm scared, so I fake like I'm doing something else. I think George is doing the same thing."

Tyler draws our attention to the illustration on the last page. "George is white instead of his usual hippo gray. When people get scared, sometimes they get pale or white."

I write their responses on the board, pointing out that they are using clues from the *seen text* as well as the *unseen text*. Seen text is anything the reader can see: words, pictures, charts, graphs, any visual cues that can be used to make meaning, anything actually on the page. Unseen text is the information that resides inside the reader's head: ideas, opinions, essential background knowledge. The unseen text is unique to each reader. I point out that they are able to make logical inferences because they are using both the seen and unseen text.

Text Bound, Outlandish, or Just Right?

When readers infer, they need a healthy dose of textual evidence combined with a moderate measure of background knowledge. If a reader relies solely on the text, his thinking is text bound. If the reader relies solely on background knowledge, his response can be outlandish.

Rick seems unable to draw an inference as he reads. In response to an assignment, he writes me a note explaining his inability to complete it: "Today, I tried to find inferences in my reading. My book didn't have any."

The next day, I share Rick's thinking with the rest of the class. Several students agree that their books don't have any inferences in them either. Some other kids snicker.

"What's so funny?" I ask.

"Books don't have inferences," scoffs Sarah. "Inferences come from the reader's head. Readers have to make them."

"That's right," I say. "Readers get to help the author create meaning. The information in the reader's head is important and it adds to the flavor of the story."

When readers first begin reading something, there's very little textual information to go on. Good readers ask themselves questions as they read, and they expect to find the answers. Sometimes these answers are in the text. Other times they are in the reader's head. Good readers search for information left by the author because they know it will help them draw inferences. The more information a reader acquires, the more accurate the inferences.

Several years ago, I supervised a reading independent study for a graduate student named Lynn, who was working toward a master's degree in art education. In return she helped me integrate art into my reading workshops. One day, the students were working on a project and becoming frustrated because they wanted their artwork to be perfect. Lynn told them that art is much more intriguing if it *isn't* perfect: "The eye fixes and finishes imperfections. Art is much more interesting if everything isn't in the picture."

And so it is with inferring. Reading is much more interesting if readers can add their own "two cents' worth" as they unite personal connections with textual evidence. Inferring makes texts multidimensional. Readers get to put their personal stamp on every text they read.

■ ■ ■ ■ ■ ■   *What Works*

1. Read aloud short pieces of fiction and nonfiction that require the reader to infer. I often use picture books because they can be read in a single class period. A few of my favorites are *Rose Blanche,* by Roberto Innocenti; *Grandfather Twilight,* by Barbara Berger; and *The Wretched Stone,* by Chris Van Allsburg. (For a detailed list of books that support comprehension strategies, see *Strategies That Work,* by Harvey and Goudvis.) Before explaining the text, give students an opportunity to explain what they think is happening. (If they write down their answers, they will more likely begin to construct meaning themselves rather than expect you to do it for them.) Then return to the text and point out evidence that supports the most probable conclusions. Explain that authors do everything for a reason and that reading material that at first seems nonsensical can usually be deciphered by participating in the read by drawing an inference.

TEACHING POINT: Good readers expect the text to make sense. They search for textual evidence to support their conclusions. They trust that the author has provided essential information for them to be able to construct meaning.

2. Distinguish differences between an opinion and an inference. Provide examples and point out that sometimes opinions are based on facts, but

not always. Opinions are important but are usually driven by emotion. They aren't sufficient when interpreting text. Try using the expression *What words or pictures in the text help you draw that conclusion?* To help students distinguish differences between words that are similar in meaning, share the following definitions:

Prediction: A logical guess based on the facts. It is either confirmed or disproved by the text.

Inference: A logical conclusion based on background knowledge and clues in the text. Inferences are not explicitly confirmed in the text.

Assumption: A fact or statement taken for granted. Assumptions may or may not be based on facts or information and may or may not be correct.

Opinion: A belief or conclusion that isn't necessarily based on facts or information. It can be informed or ridiculous, because it is based on what one thinks instead of what is proven by facts to be true.

TEACHING POINT: Good readers know the difference between an inference and an opinion. When inferring, they rely on information provided in the text to substantiate their thinking.

3. List textual evidence and next to the evidence demonstrate how background knowledge helps you interpret what the evidence means. Use a double-entry diary and let students try it on their own. On the left-hand side of the paper write *textual evidence*. On the right-hand side write *background knowledge and experiences*. Stress that the right-hand side is for recording background knowledge and experiences that help interpret what the textual evidence means.

TEACHING POINT: Good readers aren't afraid to use their background knowledge and personal experience to make sense of textual evidence.

4. Teach students how to infer. I teach my students four concrete steps that encourage text-bound readers to move beyond the words:
   1. Ask yourself a question. Wonder about something in the text. (Example: What happened to the boy in *I Never Knew Your Name*?)
   2. Consider textual evidence left by the author that may represent important clues. (Example: He's always alone. He's on the roof frequently. An ambulance comes at night. People say, "What a shame.")
   3. Think about what you know about the evidence. What does your background knowledge tell you about these clues? (Example: Often lonely people feel sad. The roof is a dangerous place to be. Ambulances come when something bad happens. People often remark what a shame suicide is.)

4. Using the clues in the text and your background knowledge about the topic, try to answer the original question. (Example: The boy killed himself by jumping off the roof.)

TEACHING POINT: Good readers wonder about their reading. They use textual evidence and background knowledge and experiences to help them answer their questions.

"What's the Plan?"

Am I supposed to do these strategy things consciously or unconsciously? Because if I'm supposed to do them without thinking, I'm in trouble.

Sarah, grade 12

How is visualizing supposed to help me read a lease? How do I visualize the concept of 15 percent and words like *whereby* and *therefore* and *heretofore*? Visualizing isn't going to help me create meaning. I need to do something else to help me read hard stuff.

Jeremy, grade 12

Readers need to construct their own meaning. In order to do this, they need to apply reading strategies—consciously at first, but eventually it becomes more automatic. For the time being, Sarah must force herself to make connections, ask questions, draw inferences, and visualize. She must determine what is important versus what is just interesting. She needs to synthesize what she reads. Being aware of what good readers do will help Sarah make sense of text.

Jeremy recognizes that readers must use a variety of reading strategies. He has learned that one strategy by itself won't work in every instance. For example, visualizing won't help him understand abstract words. He needs another strategy. When students have a variety of strategies from which to choose, they have a better chance of comprehending challenging text on their own.

Strategies are intentional plans that enable readers to construct meaning. They are flexible and can be adapted to meet the demands of the material. Jeremy thinks, Hmm, visualizing isn't helping me understand what I am reading. Maybe I should try to make a connection to something I already know. Readers who do this are in charge of their reading.

Lindsay is an excellent reader who claims she doesn't consciously need to apply strategies when she reads, that she does it automatically. "When I read, I do this stuff without thinking. I don't need to make myself visualize. I'm already doing it." Good readers like Lindsay do indeed use reading strategies automatically when the material is easy. She is fine as long as she never has to read anything challenging.

When Lindsay encounters difficult text, however, meaning can break down. I assign "The Leeshore," the famous six-inch chapter from *Moby-Dick*. This is a short but difficult chapter that students often don't comprehend. Lindsay admits she doesn't understand what she read. She read the words but got stuck. I suggest that she consciously force herself to visualize as she rereads the chapter. "This time," I say, "try picturing where the characters are, what the weather is like, and who is involved in the action."

When I read difficult material, like a science journal or a VCR manual, I need help. Reading the words isn't enough. I have an advantage over a poor reader because I know several ways to get out of a difficult reading situation. One strategy doesn't work all the time. Purpose and task demand that strategies be flexible and adaptable. When I face a challenging piece of text, I assess where I might encounter difficulty. I decide what strategies to use and how I will use them. In order to understand what I am reading, I consciously think about and react to the situation at hand. Each text is different; in order to read well, I must use a variety of strategies.

Strategies take time to teach. They also take time to use. Readers who think about their reading need more time than readers who just say the words. Laura, a senior, signs up for one of my courses in hopes of improving her reading. Halfway through the semester she complains, "All this thinking while I read is slowing me down, and the only reason I took the class was to learn how to be a faster reader." Laura is equating good reading with fast reading. She may be reading more slowly but her ability to comprehend has increased dramatically.

Reading teachers can do more than *measure* comprehension. With direct, explicit instruction that demonstrates what good readers do, struggling readers can be taught *how* to comprehend text better. There is no set of prescribed activities in this book. There are no lesson plans touting a panacea for poor readers. There are only simple suggestions that can be used with young and older children alike. The access tools discussed here allow readers to set a purpose for their reading and hold on to their thinking as they process text.

Comprehension is messy. There is no clear-cut path that the brain takes when making sense. There are many roads the mind can travel as it burrows through layer after layer of meaning. Good readers don't read every document, book, or magazine article the same way. They are aware of their thinking and consciously apply reading strategies that will help them cope with the demands of the task.

Why Teach Strategies?

Teachers often wonder why they should teach students how to use comprehension strategies when there isn't enough time to cover the course material. A few benefits of strategy instruction are:

1. The entire class can work on the same strategy. More capable readers use more sophisticated text, while less able readers use simpler text. If teachers focus on what good readers do, the entire class can improve their reading. It is not too late for struggling middle and high school readers to be taught how better to comprehend what they read.

2. Strategies are applicable to all curriculum areas. A story frequently told in my part of Colorado features Nelson and his first-grade teacher, Colleen Buddy. One day Nelson asked his teacher, "Mrs. Buddy, how come in math you ask us to estimate, and in science we hypothesize, and in reading we predict? Aren't these all the same strategies?" Nelson helps us realize that comprehension strategies are really thinking strategies and are used in every aspect of our lives.

3. Teachers don't have to be reading specialists to teach comprehension strategies. They simply have to be aware of their own processes as readers. They can notice their own thinking as they read, determine what they do to make meaning, and pass these techniques on to their students.

Strategies overlap. I don't neglect one that has been previously taught when I begin a new one, and I don't continue focusing on one that students have mastered. When I move from teaching students how to use background knowledge to teaching them how to question the text, I don't ignore background knowledge. I focus my *instruction* on the new strategy, zeroing in on how to do it. In real life reading strategies have to be used simultaneously.

My reading workshops are made up predominately of struggling readers, and there is no mandated curriculum. I have the luxury of letting my students inform my instruction. Sometimes I spend two weeks on a strategy, sometimes I spend two months. My students let me know when it is time to move on. I also use a variety of genres so students can apply their thinking to different types of text. Finally, I offer them lots of opportunities to discuss and write about their thinking.

In *world literature* I do have required curriculum to teach. I can't spend six or eight weeks focusing on one strategy, nor would I want to. I must weave strategy instruction into the curriculum. Below are two quick examples of ways I have tried to do so.

Example 1

Content: Preview the world literature textbook

Lesson: Examine the organization of the textbook. What structures aid the reader? Are there footnotes, time lines, visual aids, and biographical information that can aid comprehension?

Strategy: Good readers preview their reading. They get a sense of how the material is organized and decide how to take advantage of organizational structures.

Activity: Divide the class into groups. Assign one section of the book to each group to preview. Each student individually jots down organizational structures found in that section. As a group they decide which five are the most important ones to share with the class. Record all structures on chart paper so everyone can refer to them.

Benefit: Students get an overall sense of the textbook's organization. They know what structures are in place to help them use the book more efficiently.

Example 2

Content: The Divine Comedy, by Dante

Lesson: Discuss the plot structure of the "Inferno." How does Dante begin his descent into hell?

Strategy: Good readers stop and think about what they know. They use the information to help them understand new information.

Activity: When students become confused and are unable to retell what they read, I ask them to go back to a part in the text that makes sense to them. They mark the place with a sticky note and then jot down what they know about this part. Then they take their thinking to the next level by asking a question about what they read.

Benefit: Students are surprised that thinking about what they know can help them ask questions and clear up confusions. Many students who encounter difficult text continue reading and reading until they are thoroughly confused. Getting students to think about what they know in order to frame a question or draw a conclusion can often help them clear up their confusion. This activity also gives me insight into my students' thinking. It is a powerful assessment tool.

The End Is Just the Beginning

Middle and high school literacy instruction is at a crossroads. Tomorrow's citizens face greater reading demands than ever before. The written word is no longer restricted to paper form. Children of all ages are being bombarded with information from the Internet and other electronic forms of print. The "E"-generation needs to comprehend more than ever before. Readers of tomorrow must do more than memorize words. They must be prepared to analyze, validate, and ask the next logical question. They have to know how to think.

Debates about literacy instruction rage on. The battles for greater student literacy must be fought in classrooms and can be only be won by teachers, administrators, and parents who understand the complexities of reading.

Part 3

ACCESS TOOLS

 Double-Entry Diaries

 Comprehension Constructors

 Coding Sheets

A   Double-Entry Diaries

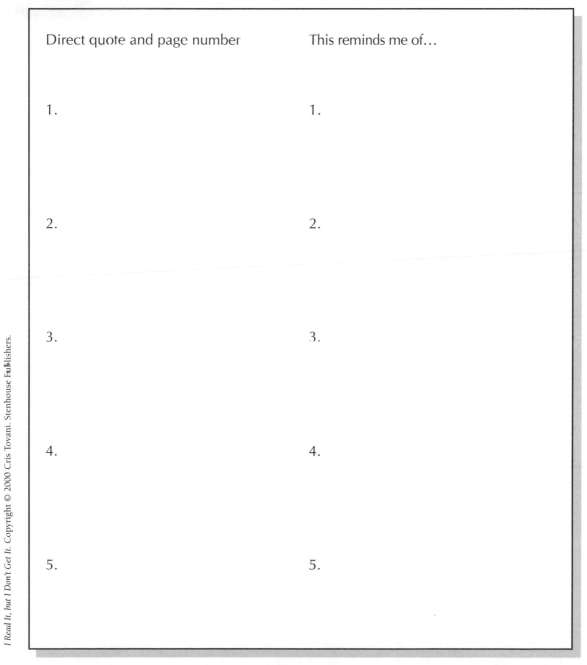

Direct quote and page number	This reminds me of…
1.	1.
2.	2.
3.	3.
4.	4.
5.	5.

Direct quote and page number   I wonder…

1.

1.

2.

2.

3.

3.

4.

4.

5.

5.

Direct quote and page number	I visualize…
1.	1.
2.	2.
3.	3.
4.	4.
5.	5.

Direct quote and page number	I'm confused because...
1.	1.
2.	2.
3.	3.
4.	4.
5.	5.

Interesting Details	Summary of Learning
1.	
2.	
3.	
4.	
5.	
6.	
7.	
8.	
9.	
10.	

What's important or interesting to me	Author's message (what is the author trying to say?)

B Comprehension Constructors

What's Your Thinking?

What are you wondering?

_____

_____

_____

What do you think might be a possible answer to your question?

_____

_____

_____

What connections can you make?

_____

_____

_____

Tips for Reading a Poem

1. Read the poem all the way through, twice.

2. Think about any background knowledge that you have that will help you connect to the people, animals, or objects in the poem.

3. Try to make a picture in your head of what's happening in the poem.

(Insert poem)

4. What do you think the poem is about?

Textual evidence   Background knowledge

Time to Draw Some Inferences

Name:

Choose a question from your reading that hasn't been answered to your satisfaction. Record the question below. Then, using the clues in the text, add any background knowledge you have to supply an inference. Remember many of these questions don't have one right answer. Be brave!

1. Record a question you have from your reading that you are most curious about.

2. Go back to the text and record any textual evidence that might help you answer your question

3. Combine the clues in the text with your background knowledge and try to answer the question you asked in number 1.

Time to Draw Some Inferences

1. Question from *The Giver*: What does it mean to be released?

2. Textual evidence:

   • Old people are released.

   • People who make mistakes are released.

   • Sick babies or twins are released.

   • Sometimes it is an honor and sometimes it is a disgrace to be released.

   • If you don't like your job, you can ask to be released.

   • Jonas got into trouble when he jokingly asked that Asher be released.

   • Only a few people have seen what happens when someone is released.

   • The community doesn't seem disturbed by certain releases.

3. Based on clues from the text, I think being released means a person is sent to another community to live out their lives.

Text-to-Self Connections

In the space below, copy a sentence or two from the text and then write down the corrections you made between the quotations and your own life. Be as specific as possible:

1. Text Quote:

This reminds me of…

2. Text Quote:

This reminds me of…

3. Text Quote:

This reminds me of…

Text Connections

Name:

Hour:

1. When I read _____

_____

I make the connection _____

_____

2. When I read _____

_____

I make the connection _____

_____

3. When I read _____

_____

I make the connection _____

_____

Silent Reading Record

Name:

Read for 30 minutes and then stop and complete the following:

1. What did you read? (Include title and page numbers.)

2. In four or more sentences summarize what you read.

3. As you were reading, what were you thinking? Write at least four sentences. Did you make any connections? What were you wondering? What opinions do you have about what you read?

Name:

Hour:

1. Read "Man at the Well."

2. As you read the piece, you will have questions. Jot the questions you have in the margins where the questions arise. You should have at least three questions.

3. After finishing the piece, write a response. It should be at least a paragraph long with no less than four sentences.

4. Notice the questions you asked. Write the three best ones below and then decide where the answers to the questions could be found: in the text, in the reader's head, in another source.

   a)

   b)

   c)

5. What do you know about: war, Vietnam, the elderly, bullies? Jot down background knowledge you have about any of the above topics.

Name:

Hour:

1. I'm stuck (copy from the text and record page number) _____

_____

I think I am stuck because _____

_____

I will try to get unstuck by _____

_____

I think I understand _____

_____

2. I'm stuck (copy from the text and record page number) _____

_____

I think I am stuck because _____

_____

I will try to get unstuck by _____

_____

I think I understand _____

_____

Name:

Hour:

1. Read *I Never Knew Your Name.*

2. How did the story end? What happened?

Textual evidence   Background knowledge

Connect To

Name:

Record the connections you made on sticky notes below. Record the words and the page number where your connection occurred. Explain the connections you made.

1.

2.

3.

4.

Example for Connect To

1. *I connect to* p. 59. *The words say,* " . . . I looked up to the Lord and wasn't all that happy with Him." *This part reminds me* of the way I felt when I heard my nephew had cancer again. *This connection helps me* sympathize with Sarney. I know what she is going through.

Comprehension Constructor for Questioning and Identifying Confusions

As you read the text complete the following:

1. Record three questions from your reading that you think are interesting.

a)

b)

c)

2. Highlight places in the text that are confusing.

3. After you finish reading, record what you remember.

4. Did you find any answers to your questions? Write down what you found out.

Inner-Voice Sheet

Name:

Book title:

Begin on page _____. Write at least four sentences per box. Decide if the voice inside your head helped you interact with the text or if it distracted you from the text. Write *interacting* or *distracting* below each section depending on what you heard.

Inner voice on page _____.   Inner voice on page _____

Inner voice on page _____   Inner voice on page _____

Coding Sheets

"Who Is Dead in the White House?"

- Before you begin to read, write down everything you know about Abraham Lincoln on the page next to the beginning of the piece.

- Highlight confusing parts. Next to each highlighted section, list at least one fix-up strategy you used to construct meaning.

- List five important facts.

  1.

  2.

  3.

  4.

  5.

- Write three important questions.

  1.

  2.

  3.

- Write a complete and thoughtful response.
(Write your response on the last page of the piece.)

Coding Sheet

Name:

- Mark at least five places in the text with the code BK. In the margin next to the words that remind you of something in your background knowledge, describe the connection.

- Mark at least five places in the text with a question mark. In the margin next to the words that cause you to wonder, write the question you have. You may begin your question with the words "I wonder."

- Highlight any parts in the text that cause you confusion. Next to the highlighted areas, describe the fix-up strategy you used to get unstuck. You may use more than one strategy.

- Summarize this piece.

- On the back, write a response to this piece.

Coding for Visualizing

Name:

Hour:

- Highlight five words or phrases that help you get a picture in your head.

- Write three questions you have about the piece. Begin each question with the words "I wonder."

- On the back of this sheet, write what you think happened in the piece.

Works Cited

Albom, Mitch. 1997. *Tuesdays with Morrie.* New York: Dell.

Alighieri, Dante. 1991. "Inferno." In *Prentice Hall Literature: World Masterpieces,* 622–44. Englewood Cliffs, NJ: Prentice-Hall.

Berger, Barbara. 1984. *Grandfather Twilight.* New York: Putnam & Grosset.

Brown, Margaret Wise. 1947. *Goodnight Moon.* New York: Harper.

Cisneros, Sandra. 1991. *The House on Mango Street.* New York: Vintage.

Cleary, Beverly. 1968. *Ramona the Pest.* New York: Morrow.

Conrad, Joseph. 1902. *Youth: A Narrative and Two Other Stories.* London: Blackwood and Sons.

Davey, Beth. 1983. "Thinking Aloud: Modeling the Cognitive Processes of Reading Comprehension." *Journal of Reading* 27: 44–47.

Dole, J. A., G. G. Duffy, L. R. Roeller, and P. D. Pearson. 1991. "Moving from the Old to the New: Research on Reading Comprehension Instruction." *Review of Educational Research.* 61: 239–264.

Fast, Howard. 1961. *April Morning.* New York: Crown.

Fielding, Linda C., and P. David Pearson. 1994. "Reading Comprehension: What Works." *Educational Leadership* 52 (February): 62–68.

Freedman, Russell. 1987. *Lincoln: A Photobiography.* New York: Clarion.

Garland, Sherry. 1994. *I Never Knew Your Name.* Boston: Houghton Mifflin.

Grahame, Kenneth. 1908. *The Wind in the Willows.* London: Methuen.

Graves, Donald. 1991. *Build a Literate Classroom.* Portsmouth, NH: Heinemann.

Haley, Alex. 1964. *The Autobiography of Malcolm X.* New York: Ballantine.

Harvey, Stephanie. 1998. *Nonfiction Matters: Reading, Writing, and Research in Grades 3–8.* Portland, ME: Stenhouse.

Harvey, Stephanie, and Anne Goudvis. 2000. *Strategies That Work: Teaching Comprehension to Enhance Understanding.* Portland, ME: Stenhouse.

Hemingway, Ernest. 1952. *The Old Man and the Sea.* New York: Simon & Schuster.

Hersey, John. 1946. *Hiroshima.* New York: Random House.

Houston, Pam. 1999. *A Little More About Me.* New York: W. W. Norton.

Hubbard, James Maurice. 1959. *Robin Red Breast.* New York: Firth, Pond.

Janeczko, Paul. 1990. *The Place My Words Are Looking For.* New York: Macmillan.

Keene, Ellin O., and Susan Zimmermann. 1997. *Mosaic of Thought: Teaching Comprehension in a Reader's Workshop.* Portsmouth, NH: Heinemann.

Keene, E., et al. In press. *Public Education Business Coalition 2000 Platform.* Denver, CO: Public Education and Business Coalition.

Kingsolver, Barbara. 1988. *The Bean Trees.* New York: Harper & Row.

London, Jack. 1981. "To Build a Fire." In *The Unabridged Jack London,* ed. by Lawrence Teacher and Richard E. Nicholls. Philadelphia, PA: Running Press.

Lowrey, Janette Sebring. 1942. *The Poky Little Puppy.* New York: Simon & Schuster.

Lowry, Lois. 1993. *The Giver.* New York: Simon & Schuster.

Marshall, James. 1976. *George and Martha Rise and Shine.* Boston: Houghton Mifflin.

Meichebaum, D., and J. Asnarow. 1979. "Cognitive Behavior Modification and Metacognitive Development: Implications for the Classroom." In *Cognitive Behavioral Interventions: Theory Research and Procedures,* ed. by P. Kendall and Hollon, 11–35. New York: Academic Press.

Melville, Herman. 1851. *Moby-Dick.* New York: Harper.

Morrison, Toni. 1987. *Beloved.* Thorndike, ME: Thorndike Press.

O'Brien, Tim. 1969. *If I Die in a Combat Zone Box Me Up and Ship Me Home.* New York: Dell.

O'Dell, Scott. 1960. *Island of the Blue Dolphins.* Boston: Houghton Mifflin.

Ogle, Donna. 1986. "K-W-L: A Teaching Model That Develops Active Reading of Expository Text." *The Reading Teacher* 39: 564–70.

Paris, S. G., M. Y. Lipson, and K. K. Wixon. 1983. "Becoming a Strategic Reader." *Contemporary Educational Psychology* 8: 293–316.

Paulsen, Gary. 1993. *Nightjohn.* New York: Dell.

———. 1997. *Sarney: A Life Remembered.* New York: Random House.

Pearson, P. David, and M. C. Gallagher. 1983. "The Instruction of Reading Comprehension." *Contemporary Educational Psychology* 8: 317–344.

Pearson, P. David, L. R. Roehler, J. A. Dole, and G. G. Duffy. 1992. "Developing Expertise in Reading Comprehension." In *What Research Has to Say About Reading Instruction,* ed. by J. Samuels and A. Farstrup. Newark, DE: International Reading Association.

Pichert, J. W., and R. C. Anderson. 1977. "Taking Different Perspectives on Story." *Journal of Educational Psychology* 69: 309–315.

Raphael, T. E., C. A. Wonnacottm, and P. D. Pearson. 1986. *Increasing Students' Sensitivity to Sources of Information: An Instructional Study in Question-Answer Relationships.* Technical Report No. 284. Urbana: Center for the Study of Reading, University of Illinois.

Rumelhart, D. 1976. *Toward an Interactive Model of Reading.* Technical Report No. 56. San Diego: University of California Center for Human Information Processing.

Rylant, Cynthia. 1993. *I Had Seen Castles.* Orlando, FL: Harcourt Brace.

Silven, M., and M. Vauras. 1992. "Improving Reading Through Thinking Aloud." *Learning and Instruction* 2 (2): 69–88.

Sparks, Beatrice. 1979. *Jay's Journal.* New York: Simon & Schuster.

Suess, Dr. 1958. *Yertle the Turtle and Other Stories.* New York: Random House.

Thornton, Lawrence. 1987. *Imagining Argentina.* New York: Doubleday.

Tolstoy, Leo. 1889. *Anna Karenina.* New York: T. Y. Crowell.

Van Allsburg, Chris. 1991. *The Wretched Stone.* Boston: Houghton Mifflin.

Wadworth, Olive A. 1938. *Over in the Meadow: An Old Nursery Rhyme.* New York: Harper.

Whimby, A. 1985. *Intelligence Can Be Taught.* New York: Dutton.

White, E. B. 1952. *Charlotte's Web.* New York: Harper & Row.

White, Ruth. 1988. *Belle Prater's Boy.* New York: HarperCollins.